The Chakmas

The Chakmas
Life and Struggle

By

S.P. Talukdar

GYAN

Published by

GYAN

Gyan Publishing House
5, Ansari Road
Daryaganj, New Delhi-110002
Phone: 011-47034999, 9811692060
E-mail: books@gyanbooks.com

Distribution Network
gyanbooks.com
India, USA, Canada, UK, Australia, France

ISBN : 978-81-212-0212-1 (HB)
First Published, 1988

2nd Impression 2022

Printed at: Gyan Press, Delhi.

THE CHAKMAS
Author: S.P. Talukdar

Foreword

The Civil Service, in India as also in other countries of the world, has the distinction of throwing up many authors of repute who have produced absorbing and informative literature. Many administrators and civil servants are credited with literary works of permanent value. Shri S. P. Talukdar, an officer of the Mizoram Civil Service, has kept up this tradition through his book on the Chakmas. He has brought out an authentic document on the history, culture and social life of the Chakmas who are little known and far less written about. He delved deep into the life and culture of this community, to which, incidentally, Shri Talukdar belongs, and brings out a plethora of interesting information which will greatly supplement our sketchy knowledge of the Chakmas.

For years the Chakmas roamed around in the Arakan region, later spread to Assam and to areas near the Bay of Bengal and finally came to settle down in the Chittagong Hill Tracts. The partition of the country disturbed them both physically and mentally. For long years they were in doldrums and even today many of them have not been able to live a permanent settled life. Shri Talukdar's book will help us to know the Chakmas better and to appreciate their problems in the proper perspective. I have no doubt that readers in general will find the book most useful.

GOVERNOR MIZORAM
RAJ BHAWAN
AIZAWL
April 29, 1987.

Sd/-
HITESWAR SAIKIA

Message

I understand that Mr. S. P. Talukdar, an Officer of Mizoram Civil Service has brought out a book on the history, culture and social life of the Chakmas who are little known and far less written about. Though I have not gone through the book yet I hope this book will help us to know the Chakmas better and appreciate their problems in the right perspective.

CHIEF MINISTER
MIZORAM
Dated 13th May, 1987.

Sd/-
(LALDENGA)

Preface

During my long tenure in government service, I have met people of different states of our country on different occasions. They were drawn from all walks of life; politicians, government servants, students, academics, businessmen, journalists and even ordinary men. From the informal chats as also serious discussions with these people and also from some recent reports appearing in national and international media on the Chakma Shanti Bahini (an underground liberation organisation operating in Chittagong Hill Tracts in Bangladesh) I gather an unmistakable impression that there are many wrong notions, mostly bred by ignorance, prevailing about the problem of Chakmas.

What accounts, in main, for the prevalence of this state of affairs is that no systematic and comprehensive study of this little known tribe has been undertaken so far. This has resulted in circulation of wrong ideas, distorted facts, half-truths and in the delineation of a picture of this tribe diametrically opposite to the reality. Till date no intellectual effort has also been directed towards gathering a systematic knowledge of this tribe—their origin and historical past, educational and cultural status, socio-economic conditions, various problems faced by them and of course the aims and objectives of the "Shanti Bahini".

This actuated me to prepare and present to the world a factual account of the different aspects of the life of Chakmas. Hence the present book.

In this book, I have put my best efforts to present a detailed description of the various facets of the life of the Chakmas mostly inhabiting the eastern parts of our country (the States of Tripura, Assam, Arunachal Pradesh and Mizoram) as also the Chittagong Hill Tracts in Bangladesh and Arakan in Burma.

On account of the great geo-strategic significance of their habitation, the Chakmas' issue has become a serious concern to three different countries namely India, Bangladesh and Burma. India being a federal country, all the states of the Indian Union are also exercised about the problem of the Chakmas.

The root of their present problem, in fact, lay in the partition of India in 1947 and as a result of which the Chittagong Hill Tracts, the home-land of the Chakmas, were merged with Pakistan without first ascertaining the wish of its inhabitants. Subsequently, time to time, they had to leave their native place i. e. the Chittagong Hill Tracts and cross over international boundary to enter India and Burma. Ever since they have been branded as 'Nomads', 'Bengali Chakmas', 'Refugees', 'Foreigners' and 'Trespassers' by political leaders, administrators and even by some scholars.

Frankly speaking, I wonder how much justice do we do to them when we raise so many doubts about the Chakmas and sometime also paint a dark picture of them. Various questions generally heard about them are : Who are these people ? How and why they turned homeless ? Are they really the refugees in India ? What ethnic threat are they facing ? It was my strong desire to search probable answers to all such questions that led me to undertake a study of the Chakmas, to which incidentally I also belong. I have tried to be as much objective in my study as possible though subjectivity may not be completely ruled out in such type of work.

In the course of preparation of this study and collection of reference material I was helped by many of my friends and well-wishers to all of whom I pay my sincere thanks. Particularly, I would like to express my deep sense of gratitude to Mrs. Kalyani Maitra of National Library, Calcutta without whose cooperation and guidance in the collection of reference books this work would not have been completed.

My sincere thanks are also due to His Excellency Sri Hiteswar Saikia, the Governor of Mizoram, who very kindly went through the script and also helped me throughout in the publication of this book.

Last but not the least thanks are also due to my wife Smt. Bindu Lata Talukdar for her untiring help, love and cooperation in fulfilling this mission.

S. P. TALUKDAR

Contents

List of Illustrations and Maps

ILLUSTRATIONS

MAPS

Abbreviations

CHT	Chittagong Hill Tracts
AP	Arunachal Pradesh
CEM	Chief Executive Member
MDC	Member District Council
CDC	Chakma District Council
MNF	Mizo National Front
PC	People's Conference
NEFA	North Eastern Frontier Agency
BSF	Border Security Force
CRPF	Central Reserve Police Force
JSS	Jana Samhati Samity
MU	Mizo Union

INTRODUCTION
A BRIEF CHRONOLOGY OF CHAKMA HISTORY

About 5000 B.C. and earlier

It is a rather difficult task to present a chronological and lucid account of the history of the Chakmas though the dates are not missing altogether. From the Indian and the Chinese historical records we learn about the mass exodus of the people of different races from Central Asia who moving to West and after traversing across different lands finally settled down in Burma. The first to settle down in this manner were the people of the Tibeto-Burman Race followed by those of the Mon-Kamer Race and last to come were the Tai-Chinese people. The Tibeto-Burmans entered Bengal through the north-eastern passes and maintained a corridor link with Burma through these mountains. These passes which served as gateway to enter India for these people are still in existence.

The Burmese and the Arakanese ethnically belong to the Tibeto-Burman race. The progenitors of these tribes are known as Tsak, Shak or Thek. The Chakmas belong to a tribal clan of the Tibeto-Burman race. The distinctiveness of the people of the Tibeto-Burman race which is an inseparable part of the 5000 years old glorious Indian heritage and culture can be conspicuously noticed to this day.

About 2000 B.C.

One branch of the Shak Tribes moved gradually westward reaching Central India and established its rule in the foot-hills of the Himalayan ranges. According to the Buddhist religious beliefs, a son of the king of Benaras, Sakkyawaddi, who in his future life was to be born as Gautama Buddha, established his kingdom at Arakan. Although it is hard to establish this as a historical fact, we see that the earliest signs of the Buddhist culture are to be found among the people of this race.

About 500 B.C.

The Chief of Tha-kya (Sakya) clan Dhaja (Daza) and Raja of Kapillavasthu emigrated from Central India to live with the people of their clan in the upper region of Burma. Dhaja Raja along with his numerous followers established his kingdom first at Mara Mau-re-ya (a country West of Khyengdweng river now called the Kabaw/Kubo Valley). After sometime thence he moved and established his dominion in the country of Theng-dwai (Thiutwe) but the place did not suit him. Ultimately he moved to Male area and married the queen Na-ga-tshein (widow of Binnaka Raja) who like Dhaja Raja belonged to the Tha-kee-ya (Sakya) race. They then built the city of upper Pugan. There a son named Wee-ra-ga was born to them. The royal family once again moved to the ancient capital of the Tha-Kee-ya race of kings called Ta-goung or Theng-ga-Tha-ra ta and renamed it as Pin-tsa-ta-goung and Dhaja Raja set up a regular Government there.

About 250 B.C.

Since the conquest of Kalinga (261 B.C.), a strong and independent kingdom on the Bay of Bengal, by Asoka the Great and spread of Buddhism in South India and Ceylon, Buddhistic elements began to strike roots in lower Burma around 241 B.C. The Buddhist missionaries worked their way farther into the mountainous regions in northern Burma.

During king Asoka's reign, a prince called U Cancha Uparaja came to Arakan and led a pious monastic life which was considered highly symbolic of the rejuvenation of people's faith in Buddhism and its traditions.

5th Century A.D.

In 5th century A.D., Buddha Ghosa, a famous Buddhist sage from Gaya brought Buddhistic religious relics to Thaton in southern Burma and worked for strengthening Buddhism there. Till then the Burmese language had no alphabet or script and the Burmese for the first time adopted this script and Pallava alphabet for their written language.

11th Century A.D.

Anawratha, king of Pugan or Pagan, the kingdom established by Dhaja Raja, invaded Thaton in 1057 and carried away the sacred religious relics which were kept in a bejewelled casket along with a large number of Buddhist monks who were mainly the followers of Hinduism. Anawratha conquered Arakan and perhaps also visited southern Bengal as far as Chittagong.

13th Century A.D.

The victory of Muhammad Ghori against the Rajputs led by Prithviraj Chauhan in the second battle of Tarain (1192) paved the way of Muslim rule in the Gangetic plains of India. The establishment of Muslim rule in India resulted in the destruction of Buddhism in India which then shifted to hills in Chittagong (southern Bengal), Assam and Arakan.

14th Century A.D.

Tsakma/Sawngma (Chakma Raja) Marekyaja emigrated from Arakan to Bengal bordering Arakan area and Chittagong and established his kingdom there. The last remnants of Indian Buddhist culture were safely preserved among the inhabitants of this territory and the main source of the present day Buddhist culture in Bengal can be traced to that period.

CHAPTER 1

MEANING AND SIGNIFICANCE OF 'CHAKMA'

The word 'Chakma' or 'Chukma' (as spelt by some British scholars) is a generic term given to a predominant hill tribe of CHT dwelling in the corridor link of Arakan (Burma) by the then British administrators and scholars who ruled over and researched on these tracts of hill from mid-18th century to mid-20th century. These ethnic tribal peoples have been grouped together under a common name or head in the British census records. It takes form as under-CHAKMA TSAK-THEK (in Burma). The word 'Chakma' is, therefore, a recent appellation given to the predominant hill tribes of CHT(lying between 21° 25° and 23° 45° north latitude and between 90° 50° east longitude) by the British.[1]

It is interesting to observe here that the word Chakma in English is not pronounced as it is spelt out. Any Chakma individual generally even to this day would pronounce himself as ƆHAWNGMA or SAWNGMA by caste and not Chakma. So the English spelling of Chakma has perhaps deviated and deflected from the peculiar characteristics of its original pronunciation by which the race had been known before the English spelling came in vogue. This is nothing unusual if we take into consideration variance in spellings of many other popular names. To cite one instance only, there are many different English spellings of the famous Chinese traveller and scholar Hiuen Tsang (who travelled in India about 629-45 A.D.) e. g. Hiuen Tsang, Hiuen Tsaing, Yuan Chwang and Hiouen Thsang. Similarly the name of the race/clan in which Lord Buddha was born is spelt out as 'The-kee-ya' but pronunced as 'Sa-kee-ya' on "Sakya'. Therefore, the pronunciation of 'THEK' also corresponds to 'SAW'. In other words, Tsak or Thek is also spelt as Chaw or Saw. CHAW (SAW) is also used as Thai titles. These are still retained as the title of a prince by all the branches of the Thai family.

Now to come to the root of the word 'Ma', 'Mi' (Mian) which refers to pronoun 'I' or to noun or to nation in the Burmese and the Arakanese languages. In other words, Ma, Mi (Mian) connotes man or people. In conclusion it can be said therefore that the word CHAWNGMA or SAWNGMA or CHAKMA or CHUKMA means people of Tsak or Thek clan who are the progenitors of the Burmese race.

Various tribes such as Khyeng-tha, Khuime or Kwe, Khey, Doing-Nuk, Mroong dwell on the hills of Arakan. The British scholars support the view that the Chakmas belong to Khyeng-tha race (Mongolian family).[2]

Khyeng-tha (Arakanese word) signifies people or nation living near water. In Burmese the pronunciation Khy-Chaw i.e. Khyeng-tha→Chaw-eng-tha means Chakma.

The ancient history and the glorious past of this race still remain shrouded in obscurity as no serious and definitive study has been conducted by scholars on Chakmas.

Notes:

1. "The Chakmas, who belong to the Tibeto-Burman group of people, are Thet or Sak people according to the Burmese language. They came to the area when Burma destroyed the Arakan Kingdom, Arakanese dissidents against the Burmese administration took refuge in Chittagong Hills which

was under the British Administration." (ZO History, Chapter VIII, by Vumson).

2. "The tributary Tribes residing within the administrative boundary of Hill Tracts (Arakan) may be classified as below: Kamees or Kumees, Mros, Chins, Choungthas, Chaws, Koons.

Which of the above clans are the aborigines of hill tracts or which of them first settled there will never in all probability be known—neither tradition nor old records avail towards the solution of the question, and probably the explanation given by PEMBERTON (report on the Eastern Frontier, Calcutta 1835) when writing of the Manipuris and the way they settled in Manipur, which lies more than 2° north of the latitude of the Arakan hill tribes forming our Eastern Frontier.

He observes: Rejecting a totally unworthy of attention the Hindoo origin claimed by the Manipuris of the present day, we may safely conclude them to be descendants of a Tartar Colony, which probably emigrated from the North-West borders of China during the Sanguinar conflicts for supremacy which took place between the different members of the Chinese and Tartar dynasties in the 13th and 14th centuries.

These Mongolian hordes passing southward from Tibet in successive waves towards the sea, doubtlessly populated the Valleys of Burma and Arakan, leaving behind in the hills of our Eastern Frontier (which running down from a spur of the Himalays, and branching out into several ranges, may be roughly said to comprise the whole land from Tibet to Arakan), a succession of hill tribes consisting of Assamese and the inhabitants of Cossya, Garrow, Jyntia, Chittagong and Arakan Hills. The features of the majority of the Arakan tribes point them out as unmistakably belonging to the great Mongolian family of which the Burmese are an off-shoot and that their language, with few exceptions, is a distinct and separate one will be apparent to any Burmese scholar on reference to the small table of the more common words and phrases in Kamine which I have given in the appendix: in short any opinion is greatly against their being regarded as aboriginal tribes, unless a prescriptive right, resting on the basis of their occupation of the hill portion of our Eastern Frontier for some centuries, can entitle them to this appellation. Even within the last thirty years, practical illustration has been afforded to the gradual movement of lower tribes towards the plains under the pressure of stronger tribes above and such a condition of things existing for centuries, would clearly explain the theory propounded by PEMBERTON as to the process by which the Manipuris and other tribes have been forced far south from the higher steppes of the Himalayas and Tibet....

The Kamees, including the Mros (for they are of one family), amounting to over 10,000 form the largest division of the tribes, and some thirty years back dwelt on the mountain ranges, but were forced down towards the river banks from their highland homes in consequence of the pressure and constant raids inflicted on them by stronger tribes to the north: they are divided into twenty two clans, each with a distinct chief and name, but their forced migration has upset in a great measure the patriarchal authority and self-Government that at one time chief of clans possessed. Each village has a chief or 'Toungyamin' a title given by the Arakanese, in which language it means the Chief of a hill ('Toung' a hill, and 'Min', a Chief) a meaning which in their own language is conveyed by the word 'Maiarain'.

The Chins, who come next in order, are very scanty throughout Burma and Arakan, comprising many thousands, living mostly along the watershed of the long and extensive range of mountains known as the Yomatoung, which extends from far north, where our Eastern Frontier is coterminous with upper Burma, into British Burma as far as the Myantoung District.

The next hill race of interest are the Choungthas, who have been briefly alluded to as Arakanese stock, sent up to the hills some centuries back by order of the kings of Arakan on account of their reputed bravery, hardiness to control or rather attempts to control, the hill tribes....

Lastly came the Chaws, who are a small tribe, an off-shoot of the great Aryan family. Tradition says that they were offered as Pagoda slaves by a pious queen of Arakan named

'SAW-MA-GYEE', some three centuries back when Arakanese influence and the tenets of Buddhism extended far higher up in the hills than the limits of our present control; their duty was to keep clean in orders some Pagodas which are now more or less in ruins, their language is distinct, and unlike the aboriginal tribes, or the Choungthas, they contract marriage among their own clan....

The last diversion of our tributory tribes to be noticed is that of the Koons, a portion of whom with their Chief, Kapa, settled within our frontier line in 1875, as they could no longer withstand the frequent attacks made on them beyond the border. They appreciated the more keenly the advantages of becoming subjects of Government from having, for three or four years previously, lived sufficiently near to the British boundary. (The Hill Tracts of Arakan 1881, Chapter III, Ethnological. by Maj.W.Gywnne Hughes)

CHAPTER 2

ESTABLISHMENT OF SAKYA KINGDOM AT ARAKAN

As noted already in the Introduction that the Tibeto-Burmans were the first race of people to move from central Asia and enter India through the north-eastern passes. This racial clan appears to have moved as far as the Central India and were living there much earlier than the birth of Lord Buddha. History also records the repatriation of the people from Central India to Burma enroute southern Bengal and Arakan. This to and fro movement which set in in the distant past still continues. Many ethnic groups lost their racial purity due to intermixing of blood as a result of these movements and in the course of time passed into oblivion.

Among the earliest tribes we find the traces of 'Tha-Kya' (Sakya) clan in which the great sage Buddha was born and whose emigration from Central India was accounted by way of Arakan (southern Burma). When Abhiraja, the first Sakya Prince of Kap-pi-la-wet (Kapilavattu or Kapilavastu) entered Burma with his army as early as 903 B.C. i.e 260 years before the birth of Gautama Buddha (believed to have lived during 643-523 B.C.) he founded for the first time his Kingdom called Thenga-tha-rata (Thengat-tha-ngae or Sanga-Sarattha) in the Tagaoung (old Pagan city now lying in ruins situated on the Irrawady river on 23° 30° north latitude) in the upper valley of Irrawady.

The Arakanese chronicles claim an antiquity of their royal dynasty as far back as 2666 B.C., long long before the birth of Gautama Buddha. The Arakanese Kingdom with its capital at Ramawadi near modern Sandoway paid tribute to the King of Banarai (Benaras) who in his future life was to be born as Gautama Buddha and who reigned from Banaras and allotted to his son Kanmyin Sakkyawadi all the countries inhabited by the Burman,Shan and Maly races from Manipur to China border. Kanmyni peopled his kingdom with multitudes of non-Aryan Tribes like the Mongolian and the Lohitic from the northeast and settled the progenitors of the present Arakanese on a strip of land on Yoma mountains and they still inhabit this place. This is the conclusion arrived at by W.W. Hunter in Imperial Gazetteer.

The two sons of Sakya prince Abhiraja, Kan-radzagyee and Kan-radza-ngay contended for the throne on the death of their father. They were, however, advised by their respective counsellers not to wage wars on each other and let the succession to the throne be decided on the basis of rivalry in noble deeds. Whereupon it was decided that each should begin construction of a religious building which should be completed by the following morning and the one who succeeded in the task should ascend the throne. The younger brother engaged his people and completed the struc'ure of the building using planks and bamboos which he covered with a white cloth with some paintings thereon which invested it with the look of a finished building. The following morning when he saw that his younger brother had completed the structure of the religious building, Kan-radza-gyee, the elder brother, conceded the defeat of his people. He assembled his troops, descended the Irrawady through the mouth of Khendweny river and then crossed over Yoma—Toung range of mountains and set up a monarchical regime in North Arakan (a mountainous country) on the mountain called Kyouk-Plan-Toung east of the river Cits-Tsha-Ba or Ga-Tsha-Bha, the lower part of Kolodan. He then proclaimed himself the king of the country. The area conquered by Kan-radza-gyee is called Udigirate (Udaya-giri-rastra in Sanskrit) in Pali. In the Chakma history this king is known as Uday-giri Raja.[1]

The Sakya prince Kan-radza-gyee and his followers had at one time lived in the Arakan Yoma, a cramped and stunted extension of the great multiple congeries of mountains extending from Assam to China. This mountain passage maintains corridor links with CHT where the hill tribes have preserved their distinctive racial and ethnic character. A great majority of the hill tribes belongs to the Tibeto-Burman race and consist mostly of Chakmas and Tongchhungya. They come of the same ethnic stock.

The Sakya line of rulers continued to grow at Arakan in general and during the reign of the thirty third descendant of Abhiraja (Binnaka Raja, a contemporary of Buddha) an another wave of Sakya race moved into Arakan from upper Irrawady. On the death of Binnaka Raja—he died on the right bank of Irrawady near the present ruins of lower Sabenago (Buddhist name Vhakma Nagar and presently known as Male)—his followers were split up into three different groups which are as follows :

First group

The first group migrated eastward and founded the nineteen 'Shan States' of the eastern Burma.

Second group

The second group stayed back at Male with the chief queen of Binnaka Raja, Naga Sang.

Third group

The third group moved down the Irrawady to live with their brethren in the western country (Arakan) then ruled by a descendant of Abhiraja.

As mentioned hereinbefore, the area conquered by Kan-radza-gyee is called Udigirate in Pali (Udāya-giri-rastra in

Sanskrit) and he also founded the Kingdom of Dha-ngya-wadi or Dhanyavati in Arakan before the birth of Gautama Buddha. Here it would be better to give an extract from the historical records, the history of Arakan Kingdom, which is as follows:

The city Dha-ngya-wadi (on the East of the Ga-tsha-ba river) now Kolodan[2] in Arakan was reigned by the King Anga -dza-na, the son of Kapi-la-wot (or Magadha) and of this race fifty five kings reigned throughout a period of 1800 years, another dynasty then succeeded which numbered twenty four kings, whose reign extended throughout a period of 835 years.

Then came the king Tsan-do-thoo-Vee-ya who was not of a different dynasty but in his reign the Buddha Gautama having been in Magadha visited Arakan; the pious king in honour of Buddha Gautama built the famous temple of Maha-muni, which still exists. The ruins of the ancient temple of Mahamuni built entirely of stone, the site of the former cities, shown by the ruins of tanks and ruins of Pagodas, the extensive stone walls at the old Capital, certainly tell of more flourishing kingdom than what the British found it.

Notes:

1. Arakan was known as Rakhaing. The name is said to be derived from the Pali word Rak-pu-ra signifying abode of demons which name may have been given to this country by the Buddhist Missionaries from India. The Arakanese called the Burmese 'PYUS'.

2. The Kooladan has been explored by Europeans to nearly 300 miles from its mouth and the Lemroo to about 120 miles from its source: both of these rivers are navigable by large boats and small steamers to the centre of the hills, after which, owing to rapid water and oozing rocks, navigation become difficult and dangerous. Among these remarkable ranges of mountains one is called the 'KYOUK-PANDOUNG with a fine plateau of several miles on the top composed of sandstone and trap formation. Running almost due east and

west, this plateau extends over 13 miles, and average height being from 3000 to 4200 feet, Historical interest has also been attached to this mountain, tradition shows that it has been many centuries ago, the site of a large city, and the seat of government under a prince called the 'KAN-RAJA'. The tradition that it was at one period inhabited is corroborated by the fact that old fruit and plam trees are still growing there, and by the existence of relics of the past in the shape of a small pagoda which have been discovered on the top. A large portion of the surface is entirely denuded of all vegetation, and several acres are covered with bare rock, indented here and there with remarkable 'pot-holes' or 'giant-kettles'. These pot holes are of all sizes, ranging from four inches to three and four feet in diameter. As is generally the case with Burmese and Arakanese manuscripts which purport to relate to the history of remote past, facts of which have been freely interlarded with myths and fiction. The legend refers to a period prior to the incarnation of Gautama. But it is quite clear from the freshness of the inscription on a stone found on the top and from the wall that it has preserved the state of a small pagoda discovered there in 1872) and proves that at no very remote date, this mountain has been peopled. Some miles away to the east, on the Yomatoung which separates Arakan and Pegu, is another prominent mountain summit called 'Pogoung-Toung'. It is referred to in this story as having been a halting place for prince Kan-yaza-Gyee on his way from Irrawady to the Kooladan. It was known in the Pali language, Guttshape-nuddee river, prior to his forming the settlement of Kyouk-Pandoung (The Hill Tracts of Arakan by Maj.W.Gwynne Hughes, Chapter I, p.4).

CHAPTER 3

HOLY LAND OF MAHAMUNI (BUDDHA) IN NORTH ARAKAN

The descendants of Abhiraja and Binnaka Raja belonging to the Sakya line of kings established their kingdom in northern Arakan at Dha-Gnya-Wadi (Dhanyavati) and this has been the stronghold of a mighty creed i.e. Buddhism since ancient times. Even during the reign of Asoka the Great, in 272 B.C., a prince named U. Cancha Uparaja came to Arakan and lived there like a monk which was believed to be a great sign of rejuvenation of people's faith in Buddhistic traditions which later were firmly entrenched there.

The Indian cultural influence penetrated to Arakan (Burma through two major routes :

1. Along sea coast of Bengal (Chittagong) to Akyab, and
2. Overland through north-east India (Assam) to Pagan and stepping down along the sea routes.

The Indian influence is also clearly visible in the names of several capitals in Arakan region viz. Dhanyavati, Vesali, Sambawuti and Babbotoung. All these names originated in the classical Indian languages like Sanskrit or Pali. Vesali was named after Buddha's home land, situated in the north-east of Patna in Bihar. Therefore, north Arakan embraced in its fold cultural streams of the Aryans since very ancient times. These cultural influences were not only consolidated here, but more remarkably, also underwent further development.

The famous British scholar R. Beileau Pemberton in his report on the Eastern Frontier of British India had acknowledged that near the ancient capital Dhanyavati, there stood at the head of inferior branch of the Gat-sha-bha or Kolodyne about 50 miles from Akyab a principal city known as Babootoung.

"The principal creek near Babootoung hills throw off two branches which run through and are crossed by lofty wooden bridges ; a good deal out of repair. On the southern side of the principal street which runs east and west, are the ruins of the ancient palace and fort, consisting of the triple square enclosure of stone and brick wall, connected with lime; the stone having apparently been originally employed in the construction and the subsequent repair effected with bricks and the work altogether is of cosiderable extent, and the labour bestowed in connecting the different detached hills by curtain of stones and brick walls must have been immense. They are now in a dilapidated state and as sites more favourably situated have been selected for occupation by the civil and military authorities of the province, it can never be an object of importance to repair these works. The inhabitants of the town may be estimated at from eight to ten thousand, and they consist principally of old families of respectability who are continuously attached to the spot from local association."

This country remained isolated and cut-off from the mainstream of the world historical developments during the Christian era and would have been blotted out from human memory but for some obscure historical records. Thus it remained a closed country unknown to the modern world. For the same reason the people of Mahamuni could not play their due role in the progress of world history as compared to the people of the two other peninsulas of Asia—India and Arabia.[1] Nevertheless, many Buddhist monks of Arakan ardently believed in the rejuvenation of Buddhism and the fragile world peace on the inspiration from this ancient principal Buddhist city which now is lying in ruins in North Arakan.

At Mahamuni, in the Kyauktaw township, there is a pagoda once famous for enshrining an image of Gautama of great sanctity and which on the conquest of Arakan in 1784 by the Burmese was removed by the victors from Mahamuni to Amarapura and enshrined there. Presently it is enshrined in the Arakan pagoda of Mandalay.

It should, therefore, be now abundantly clear that the old and strong cultural traditions with which once the people of Arakan were identified so closely underwent erosion and ultimately fell into decay due to ravages of time.

Notes :

1. At the border of hill tracts from plains of Chittagong, at Rangoonia, there stands a Mahamuni Temple (in testimony of their avowal of akinness with the races of Dhangnyawadi and Babbootong where the original shrine of Mahamuni stood).

"The Mahamuni is the great festival of the year amongst the Maghs and Chakmas. It is celebrated on Bishu day, the last day of Maghee year in honour of Buddha Gautama, also called Sakya Muni, the founder of Buddhism, more correctly a great reformer of that region who lived about 550 B.C. and is the 24th Buddha an enlightened one. On this occasion the hill people combine business with pleasure and thoroughly enjoy an al-frisco picnic of three days duration. The ceremonial dates fall in the second week of April, when the days are not too hot and the nights are pleasurably cool. The principal meeting place is at temple on the estates of the Mong Raja, situated in the Regulation District of Chittagong, some two miles away from the bank of the Karnafulee river. The site of the temple could not have been better selected. It is situated at the junction of the plains and the hills, in the midst of beautiful grove of Nageswar tree (*Mesua ferrea*). These afford excellent and ample shade to all for the purpose of bivouacking. They are in full bloom at this season and fill the air with the delightful fragrance of their beautiful white flowers. As the days of the festival approach crowds of Maghs and Chakmas, in village parties numbering from five to twenty, or even more, may be met on road and river. They are jovial throng, free from care, decked in holiday attire, and brimful of glee and laughter. The fatigues of the journey are unheeded in the round of light chaff, song and dance which they beguile the tedium of the way. A drummer leads the procession, cheering any flagging spirit with vigorous tatto and in his own comical gyrations, while every few minutes the party will, in an excess of good spirits, give forth in unison the 'hoiya' or hill cry. The parties consist principally of young men and maidens with one or two staid elderly people as chaperons. The festival is distinctly for the youths, and the great majority of marriage-truth are pledged in the silent shade of the Nageswar grove. To the west of the groves stands the temple; built by Konjai, the Palaingsa Magh, in 1813. In the room, and facing main entrance sits an enormous gilded stone figure of Gautama. This entrance is so narrow that two persons can hardly pass through in abreast position, but room is meant for devotees—their Holy and Holies, around which runs a square valuted corrider some ten or twelve feet in breadth, and one hundred and sixty feet in length, which also has a narrow door way in the centre opening out into a courtyard which is walled in. The priests are seated at the feet of the huge image, on a high raised masonry platform and there they tell their beads and wait largesse from the erowd of devotees that attend the festival. Each party of hill people, as it arrives passes in front of the temple, and without entering, makes obedience to the image with folded hands and bent head, and then hurries off to secure a tree, under which to camp (Chittagong Hill Tracts by R.H. Sneyd Hutchinson).

CHAPTER 4

ASSIMILATION OF SAKYA CLAN OF CENTRAL INDIA WITH THE BURMESE

History has recorded for posterity how and why the Sakya clan of Kapilavasthu was massacred and it would be better to reproduce a passage from historical records in this regard. The passage :

> "King Prasenjit of Kosala was a great admirer of Buddha. Buddhist texts have recorded many conversations between the two. His admiration extended also to the Sakya clan in which the great master was born and asked for a daughter of a Sakya Chief as his wife. The Sakyas too proud of their lineage to enter into such an alliance, but too weak to refuse openly the request of such a powerful potentate in their immediate neighbourhood, had to resort to a trick. A slave girl in the guise of the offspring of a Sakya Chief was passed off as the legitimate daughter of the Sakya race and married to Prasenjit. A son, Wee-ta-thoo-pa or Viduadabha was born of this marriage and when he paid a visit to his maternal grandfather at Kapilavastu the true origin of his mother came to light. It natu-

rally created a great sensation and Prasenjit discarded both his queen and son. But the great Lord Buddha told him that whatever might have been the origin of the queen, the son belonged to the caste of his father and on his advice Prasenjit restored both the queen and the prince to favour."[1]

On the death of king Prasenjit, Prince Viduadabha succeeded to the throne of Kosala. He carried out massacre of the people of the Sakya clan at Kapilavasthu without regard to men, women or children. As a result of this insensate manslaughter, Dhaja Raja of Kapilavasthu (a contemporary of Binnaka Raja of Sakya clan of Burma) had to flee towards east. Though many survived this ghastly occasion, it was virtual end of the illustrious autonomous clan which produced one of the greatest teachers who ever walked on this earth.

Dhaja Raja along with his followers first founded his new Kingdom at Moriya (Mau-ra-ya), the country to the west of the Khyengdweng in Burma and now called Kuba valley.

After reigning briefly over that small kingdom, he abandoned it and founded yet another kingdom in Thiutwe (Thengdwai) in Burma. Later he left Thiutwe for Male where he met queen Naga-Tshein (widow of Binnaka Raja) and married her as she also came of the Syaka (Tha-Kee-ya) race.

A son named We-re-ga was born to them. From Male they moved to the ancient capital of the Sakya (Tha-kee-ya) kings in the Tagaung country called Ta-gaung or Theng-ga-tha-ra-to or Sanasaratha in the Tagaung country.

According to the Burmese chronicles, Dhaja Raja established his kingdom in the twentieth year of religion, while according to the Shans, in the twenty fourth year of the same. The older city founded by Abhiraja was called Tagaung and the one re-built by Dhaja Raja was named Pinjalarit (Panchalarastra or Pinja Tagoung shortened into Pagan).

In the Dhaja Raja dynasty seventeen kings succeeded in regular succession, but they reigned for a short span only. The last successor of this dynasty was Tha-de-mu-ha-radza. The king had no son. The chief queen Kein-na-ree-de-wee had a brother of the name of La-ba-doo-ha who was then appointted Ein-she-men or the Crown Prince.

This is how the Sakya clan became assimilated happily with the Burmese who are also the descendants of the same T-sak, Shek, or Thek clan.

Notes :

1. The following passage sheds light on the emigration of the Burmese from Central India and historical background of the foundation of the city of Tagoung.

> "Long before the appearance of Gautama, a king of Kauthala (Kosal, Oude) and Pinjalarit (Punjab), desiring to be connected by marriage with the king of Kauliya. sent to demand a daughter, but receiving a refusal on the ground of his being of an inferior race, he declared war, and destroyed the three cities of Kauliya, Dewadaha and Kapilawat, which were governed by the Sakya race of kings. These cities were afterwards restored, and the Sakya line was re-established ; but on the occasion of the above disaster, one of the Sakya race of kings, Abhi Raja, the king of Kapilwat, retired with his troops and followers from Central India and came and built Tagoung, which was then also styled Thengat-tha-ratha, and Thengat-thanago. Here had stood a city in the times of the three preceding Buddhas. In the time of Kekkuthan it was called Thanthayapura in that of Gaounagoun, Ratha pura and in that of Katthaba, Thendwe."
> (Burmese Maha-Radza-Wong, Vol. III)

CHAPTER 5

THE ARAKANESE SWAMP OVER TO BENGAL

The establishment of a Sakya Kingdom at Dhan-ng-wadi (Dhanyavati) in north Arakan before the birth of Gautama Buddha is confirmed by the historical records. Therefore, all the kings who succeeded in the line of kings of Arakan were the descendants of the Sakya clan. In 1052 A.D., the king of Pagan (Burma) Anawratha (Anurudha) conquered north Arakan. As a result of this abject defeat, a Sakya clan moved from north Arakan towards west and went down the rivers Matamouree, Sangoo, Thenga and Tuichong. The king of Pagan wanted to take away the image of Lord Buddha (Mahamuni image) but did not succeed in his efforts to remove the ponderous image. The sanctity of the Mahamuni image is deeply embedded in the mind of the Arakanese and this heritage can still be conspicuously observed among the people of the Sakya race.

According to the Arakanese chronicles, the kings of Bengal, Pegu, Pagan and Siam acknowledged the supremacy of Arakan when this kingdom was at the zenith of its power in 1133 A.D. But during the next century and a half, the country had to suffer heavily from the incursions made by Shans and Talaings, until king Minti of Arakan in 1294 A.D. repulsed the invaders, restored the kingdom, and in turn, marched his army against Pagan and Pegu.

At the close of the 16th century, there took place a fierce struggle between Ava and Pegu and the king of Arakan took advantage of the weakened position of his neighbours in Bengal in extending his dominion over Chittagong and northwards as far as the Meghna river (now in Bangladesh).

As already mentioned, from early 12th century onwards the people from Arakan swamped over the river valleys originating into the hills of north Arakan and gradually passed through the mountain slopes of the CHT, before reaching the plains of Chittagong which meet the Bay of Bengal here.

The conceivable history of Arakan has its beginning from King Minto who was reigning about 1374 A.D. He had usurped power from and driven away the Chakma King Marekyaja. In the line of the Arakanese Kings Narameikhala was probably Marekyaja who fled to Bengal due to the dynastic struggle for the Arakanese throne in 1404 A.D. where he was cordially received by the King Ahmad Shah of Gour.

The Nawab of Bengal Jalaluddin Mohammad gave shelter to the Chakma Raja in the southern part of Chittagong where he first established his capital at Alikadam in the upper region of Matamouree river. The fascinating Chakma ballad 'Radhamon and Dhanpati' is related to this period. Some historians, however, are of the opinion that Jalaluddin Mohammad Shah was actually a Hindu king named Jadu (1418-31) who married a Muslim girl Asmantara, became converted to Islam and assumed a Muslim name Jalaluddin Mohammad Shah.

Marekyaja's (Narameikhla's) son fled away to Mon Talaing country (Talaing is probably derived from Telingana, a region on the Madras coast of India) and their route to Burma was down the Salween, a river in Burma. There was a Talaing exodus into Siam in the middle of 17th century. One group of the fugitive Arakan king during the reign of Minti moved down to Salween and the other group moved into Bengal.

It is conceivable that even prior to the actual move of the fugitive king his subjects/clan had already swamped in those areas. The movement of the Chakma clan from Siam to Bengal, therefore, is a historical event.

While the king and his son were in exile, the king of Ava placed a son-in-law on the throne of Arakan but the latter was assassinated by the Arakanese prince who took refuse in the Mon (Talaings) country (Talaings spread over Burma south of Henzada). The Mon forces were engaged in regular battle with the Burmese who were trying to regain their power, but as expected the fugitive king appeared with a force from Bengal under the command of Wali Shah. With a view to gaining the throne of Arakan for himself, Wali Shah held the king as prisoner by siding with the disloyal Arakanese Chieftain. They could not prevent, however, the escape of the king and having received another force, placed at his disposal by Siamud-din-Ahmed-Shah reganied the throne of Arakan in 1430. (It is, however, still a matter of controversy whether the independent Mohammadan kings of Bengal were from Hindu or Muslim line of dynasty. In the sober history the house of Raja Ganesh has been mentioned as Sahab-ud-din-Bayazid, Shah with Raja-Kan (Ganesh). Raja Ganesh was succeeded by his son Jadu, Jalaluddin-Mohammed).

This victory of the Chakmas against the Arakanese king with the help of the force provided by the Nawab of Bengal has been described in the Chakma ballad Gengkhuli. Since the Nawab was himself from a Hindu line of dynasty, he never interferred with the Buddhist faith of the Chakmas. The adoption of the Muslim names and titles by the Chakma rulers of that period was a clear mark of striking a happy middle path. The Buddhist tribal Chiefs never embraced Islam and the assumption of Muslim titles was probably done only to show their allegiance to the Nawab of Bengal. Islam, in fact, could never make a dent in the religious life of the Chakmas.

The rivers Matamouree, Sangoo, Raing Khyong, Thega and Toi-Choong (now Tuichong) all flow out from Arakan hill range (Arakan Yoma); but while flowing down stream they fall wide apart. However, they are linked together and interconnected with small streams for greater length of their journey. The hill rivers Raingkhyong, Thega and Tuichong join together down stream and their common flow is known as Karnafulee. (The river Raingkhyong meets Karnafulee near Chandoogona/Chandraghona and the river Thega meets Karnafulee at its watershed at a bend at Demagiri where the other hill river Tuichong also joins in.) These mountain glens and hill slopes and river valleys were the wandering places of the Chakmas from the early 12th century and who gradually moved westward, valley to valley beyond these rivers and followed and entered into other river tracts viz. Feni, Sazek, Barharina etc. which ultimately brought them into Tripura and Assam in India.

The following are the principal river and land routes from Arakan to Chittagong followed by the people of North Arakan in their movement:

a) (Route along river Matamouree and land route)

Place	Distance (Miles)	Remarks
1	2	3
Babbootoung (in North Arakan) Maungdaw (The old Kingdom of Chakmas was at Alakadam, near Maungdaw).	14 (approximate) from Babbootoung.	The rivers Matamouree and Sangoo are almost running parallel for a greater part of distance. Therefore, the people who came down through Sangoo river also followed the same track.
Ukha	35	
Rumka	9	
Ramu	11	
Idgong	9	
Dulabazar	9	

Place	Distance (Miles)	Remarks
Chakaria	15	
Chunati	15	
Dohazari	15	
Chittagong	24	
	Total: 156 Miles	

b) Route along river Rain-Khyong)

Place	Distance (Miles)	Remarks
1	2	3
Babbootong (North Arakan) Chandoogona (Chandraghona).	95 (approximate) from Babbootoung.	The river runs east to west till it meets river Karnafulee at Chandoogona. This is one of the important tributaries of Karnafulee river.
(Old capital of Chakma Chief) Rangoonia (Rajanagar the capital of the Chakma chief at the advent of British).	12	
Raozan	10	
Chittagong	20	
	Total : 137 Miles	

c) (Route along river Thega and Tuichong)

Place	Distance (Miles	Remarks
1	2	3
Babbootong (North Arakan) Dum Dumya	60 (approximate) from Babbootong.	The two rivers Thega and Tuichong are running parallel for a greater part of distance.
Andhar Maink	35	
Thega Mukh	22	
Harina Bazar	25	
Barkal	18	
Subolong	14	
Rangamati	14	
Kalipur	12	
Raozan	12	
Chittagong	20	
	Total : 232 Miles.	

During the British period the land route between Arakan and Chittagong, onc of which was known as Captain Fergusson's route led from Edong (Idogong) via Gurjineea, at the southern extremity of the Chittagong District, across the Wylatoung and Chatteedoung ranges of hills, to the city of Arakan. The Chatteedoung Chara Pala (Ballad play) of the Chakmas clearly indicates how and when they left their home land and emigrated into Bengal. This area was predominated by the Chakmas, when Chittagong first fell into the British hands. The authorities took cognizance of the head of the Chakmas, whose residence was 35 miles away from the station Islamabad to the east, northeast (now Chittagong). Islamabad was a temporary name given by the Mughal rulers. To this day, there are considerable evidence and historical records to prove that Chakmas ruled for over 300 years from 15th century onwards in the vicinity of Chittagong. It can be unmistakably seen that the Bazar (Market) of Raozan till today is known as Rajar hut (hut means bazar—Market—of the King).

Chittagong has been in the past subjected to constant wars and raids; the external forces such as the Portuguese, the Arakanese, the Afghans, the Pathans, the Mughals and lastly the British all were embroiled in wars for supremacy over Chittagong. But none of them could hold its supremacy over Chittagong for any considerable length of time and it changed hands from one master to another in quick succession. Their struggle was confined to only the plain areas of Chittagong and the hill ranges stretching from Chittagong to Arakan remained practically unaffected from the external domination. During this turbulent phase the Chakmas swamped over from northern Arakan and moved from valley to valley and thrived to establish their rule in the close proximity of Chittagong. Before the British, the Mughal rulers had to take cognizance of the Chakma rule near Chittagong.

Chittagong (old name Saptagram) had originally formed part of the extensive Hindu Kingdom of Tippera but was conquered by the Buddhist King of Arakan in the 9th century and from that time onwards the Arakanese generally succeeded in keeping it in their possession up to 1665 A.D. The king of Arakan Sole Sing Chandra or Chulatiang Chandra carried an expedition into Bengal and set up a pillar at Saptagram which according to the Burmese traditions take the name of Sit-ta-gaung from a remark of the conqueror that 'to make war is improper'.

The Muslim (Afghan/Pathan) rule in Bengal covered roughly a period of 400 years (1200-1500 A.D.) and Chittagong was probably first conquered by Muhammadans during this period. The first 100 years saw Bengal as a dependency of the throne of Delhi while for about next 250 years Bengal was almost independent under the Muslim Sultan.

During the struggle between the Mughals and the Afghans for supremacy in Bengal, towards the close of the 16th century, Chittagong seems to have been reconquered by the Raja of Arakan who annexed it to his kingdom as a tributary province. This period in history of the Chakmas is known as "Mughar Mulluk (unruly-lawless country)". Sultan Shuja, son of Emperor Shah Jehan (1628-58), ruled Bengal with his seat at Rajmahal and is credited with to have brought the Arakanese raids under some check. It is indeed a great irony of fate that on having been defeated by Aurangzeb in the wars of succession to the Mughal throne, Shuja had to take refuge in Arakan where he along with his family were brutally done to death by the Arakanese.

In place of Sultan Shuja, Mir Jumla was put in charge of the Suba Bengal and he was succeeded by Shayesta Khan (1664-89). In 1664-65, Shayesta Khan, the Governor of Bengal, resolved to put an end to the Arakanese incursions and to this end led a huge expedition against the Arakanese Raja. This expedition resulted in the capture of some forts at the mouth of the Meghna river and storming of Chittagong town. It was besieged and taken in 1665 by the Mughals under Umed Khan who changed its name to Islamabad. In 1760, Chittagong was ceded by Mir Khan, Governor of Bengal, to the East India Company.

During the time of Shayesta Khan an independent kingdom was ruled by the Chakmas which paid no tribute or revenue to the Mughal government until Muggy year 1077 MS (1713 A.D.). The relations between the British and the Burmese had been continuously tense over the control of the land inhabited by the Mongolian tribes. At long last on 24th February, 1828 peace was established when the king of Ava (Burma) gave up his claim on the provinces of Assam, Manipur, Cachar and Jayantia and ceded the provinces of Arakan and Tenasserim to the East India Company and also agreed to pay an indemnity of one crore of rupees.

From their ancestral home in Arakan the Mongolian races from 1052 A.D. onwards swamped over Chittagong and made it to be a home land of the Chakmas. On account of their long separation from their brethren in Arakan they have embraced into their fold cultures of both the Hindu and the Muslim ruling classes in their neighbourhood. They were transformed into a new generation/race similar to the Ahoms (now Assamese) who were an offshoot of Tai-Shan-race of Burma and whose progenitors were none else than T-Sak, Shak or Thek tribes.

(The Dynastic Chronology of the Chakma Kings from 1400 A.D. onwards)

SI. No.	Name of King	Period
1.	Marekyaja	1400 A.D.
2.	Kadam Thangja	He reigned for a very short period.
3.	Taina Sureswari	1500 A.D.
4.	Janu	
5.	Sattua (Cha-tho-ai-known as Pagla Raja)	Afghan, Pathan and Mughal period.
6.	Dhanbana	
7.	Dharamya	
8.	Mogolya	
9.	Subal Khan	
10.	Fate Khan	
11.	Shere Jan Khan	
12.	Shere Must Khan	Early British period under East India Company.

SI.No.	Name of King	Period
13.	Suk Deb Roy (The last King of Mughal period. The Title Roy was conferred by the Mughals)	
14.	Shere Daulawt Khan	British period
15.	Jan Khan	
16.	Tubbar Khan	
17.	Jabbar Khan	
18.	Dharam Buksh Khan (Wife Kallendi Rani)	1812–1832
19.	Kallendi Rani	1832–1873
20.	Harish Chandra	1873–1897
21.	Bhuban Mohan Roy	1897–1933
22.	Nalinakoo Roy	1935–1951
23.	Tridib Roy (Now living in exile in Pakistan. In 1972, he was Chief delegate of Pakistan team in the U.N.)	1931

The covenanted title Raja was conferred on Chakma Chief Harish Chandra by the British Government.

CHAPTER 6

THE EARLY BRITISH PERIOD

As referred to in the foregoing Chapter V, Chittagong in 1760 changed hands from the Mughals to the East India Company by a pact concluded between Mir Khan, Nawab of Bengal and the British. Under the terms of this pact the Company received from the Mughals the western part of Nizampur Road of Chittagong (the present Dhaka Trunk Road) and the rest of Chittagong was left with the Chakma Chief, King Shere Must Khan. The Company by a proclamation dated 6th Sraban 1170 MS (1763 A.D.)[1] fixed the territorial jurisdiction of the Chakma Chief as "all the hills from the Pheni river to the Sangoo and from Nizampur road in Chittagong to the hills of the Kookie Raja." That is how Chittagong was ceded to the East India Company and the Chakmas accepted the hegemony of the British represented by the East India Company.

But this did not come about in a single day. There had been a long contention over the fixation of tributes between the Chakma Chief and the Muslim rulers of Bengal. Later on the issue was, however, settled in an amicable manner. Though the Company's demand for tribute at an enhanced rate i.e.

more than what was paid to the Mughals became a cause of annoyance to the Chakma Chief. Consequently, a long drawn out war, lasting 24 years from 1760 A.D. to 1784 A.D., was fought by the Chakma Chief against the Company. In 1771, Ramoo Khan (Dewan), a relation of the Chakma Chief rebelled against the authority of the Company and gave a call to come to his assistance to "large groups of Kookie men, who lived far in the interior parts of hills and who were not aware of the use of firearms and whose bodies went unclothed."[3]

With a view to chastising the rebellious Chakmas, the British Government launched successive major offensives against them—in 1770, 1780, 1782 and 1785, respectively. The Governor General of Bengal Warren Hastings adopted leniency and so a peace agreement was signed at Calcutta and the payment of tributes due to the Company was slashed to the minimum. The annual revenue for the hill tracts of Chittagong was fixed at Rs. 1852 till 1789.

The East India Company continued to maintain the same policy of non-interference with the Chakma hill tribes in their governing the hill tracts of Chittagong as the Mughals had been pursuing earlier. This policy of the Company is manifest from a letter which the Government wrote to Mr. Irwin, the Chief of Chittagong, on 6th May, 1784, desiring to have his opinion fully, whether by lenient measures, the inhabitants of the hills might not be induced to become peaceful subjects and cultivators of the low land.

Again, in 1829, Mr. Halhed, the Commissioner reaffirmed that "the hill tribes were not British subjects but merely tributaries and we recognised no right on our part to interfere with their internal arrangements. The near neighbourhood of a powerful and stable Government naturally brought the Chief by degree under control and every leading Chief paid to the Chittagong Collector a certain tribute or yearly gifts. These sums were at first fluctuating in amount but gradually were brought to specific and fixed limit, eventually taking the shape, not of a tribute, but of a revenue paid to the state."

After the great mutiny of 1857 which shook the foundation of British rule in India, the British Government assumed direct control of the administration in India in every respect putting an end to the East India Company's rule. Since 1846, however, the revenue of CHT was raised to Rs. 11,803 per annum.

During the period of the East India Company, the Chakma Chief, Raja Dharam Buksh Khan had ruled over his subjects from 1812 to 1832. On the historic occasion when the British Monarch took over the control of the Indian administration from the East India Company, the Chakmas were under the rule of Kallendi Rani (1832-1873), the widow queen of Raja Dharam Buksh Khan.[3]

The British Government recognised her succession to the Chakma throne and her rule over her clan. She was a very capable ruler and it was during her rule that a group of upper class of Chakmas were maintaining constant cultural interactions with their neighbours in the plains. She not only ruled her people with great ability but also stood in defiance of the British Government. During her 40 years' rule she never had any rapprochement with the British, though she stood by the side of the British when some of the sepoys of the native regiments mutinied in the wake of the revolutionary uprisings all over the country in 1857 to shake off the British yoke.

The great merits of Kallendi Rani were acknowledged even by her opponents as will be evident from the following remark of a British scholar :

> "In 1857, the Kallendee Rani delivered up some of the sepoys of the native regiment that mutinied at Chittagong and had betaken themselves to the hills to avoid retribution, otherwise, for forty years she proved a thorn in the side of the Government. She was an exceedingly able woman having surrounded herself with Bengalee lawyers from Chittagong. She exercised a very great influence over her tribe and was generally feared. In 1872, she assisted in supplying coolie transport to the Lushai expedition and for this service the rent was reduced to Rs. 1,081.4 and his grandson Harish Chandra was vested with the title of Ray

Bahadur and presented with a gold watch and a chain.[4]"

Being a woman Kallendi Rani during her long reign had to encounter a stiff opposition from the men of rank in her community. Moreover, she bore no issue throughout her life. Some nobles and Chieftains in her kingdom hatched a conspiracy against her with the insidious motive of gaining the favour of the local British representative but met with little success in their nefarious designs. A noble named Nilo Chandra Dewan openly revolted against her whereat the Rani had to seek help of the Kookies and the Lushais to crush the revolt of Nilo Chandra Dewan. There was a great dismay in the community due to these internal convulsions as a result of which some people emigrated to neighbouring Tripura Kingdom. Successively in 1847, 1848, 1859 and 1860 the Kookies committed murderous outrages on British subjects residing in the districts of Tripura and CHT. The British have called this event the "Great Kuki Invasion."[5,6]

Therefore, with a view to protecting the hill subjects from the aggressions of the frontier tribes, the Lieutenant Governor recommended that the whole country of Chittagong be removed from the operation and that an Officer to be called Superintendent of the Jhum tract be appointed. Consequent upon this the constitution of the Chittagong hill tracts was framed by an act of 1860 which enabled the British Government to give the hill subjects of Chittagong some kind of administration. Following this in July 1860, a Superintendent of the hill tribes was appointed to be in Charge of the hills, which was henceforth to be known by the name of the "Hill Tracts of Chittagong". Therefore, Kallendee Rani was the last independent ruler of the Chakmas. Under the act of 1860, the hill tracts of Chittagong were divided into the following three circles :

(a) Chakmas Circle;

(b) Bohmang Circle;

(c) Maung Circle.

Each circle was headed by a Chakma, a Bohmang and a Maung Chief respectively. Originally, there was a southern circle under the subjection of the Bohmang, Chief of Burmese extraction ; a Central Circle inhabited chiefly by the Chakma tribe and a northern circle inhabited by the Burmese speaking clans with a sprinkling of immigrants from Tripura district who paid annual tribute to the British government through a Burmese Chief known as the Mong Raja. The reason of this division was that the British government was not in favour of the strong power of the Chakma Chief who held sway over these hill tribes. On the other hand, the British government was feeling increasingly concerned about the political and administrative affairs of these hill tracts. The British authorities aimed firstly to lay the foundation of administration in a restricted manner with the following basic objectives :

(1) To keep supervision on the rule of the Chakma Chief and also to curtail some of his powers ;

(2) To protect the British subjects from the Kookie menace ; and

(3) To preserve peace in the frontier areas.

In 1866, Capt. T.H. Lewin was posted as the Superintendent of the district and in 1867 the official designation was changed from "Superintendent of Hill Tracts" to the 'Deputy Commissioner Of The Tracts' and full control of all matters pertaining to both revenue and justice throughout the hill tracts was vested in his office. The British Deputy Commissioner T.H. Lewin enjoyed his association with the dwellers of the hill tracts a great deal and paid them warm compliments in his book "A Fly On The Wheel".

"I had often heard of the vicious excess and drunken debauchery of the savage races for aught I know this may be the case of the coast of Africa or New Guineas; but here in the hill tracts, throughout the three days' carnival I have not seen one drunken man not witnessed any discourtesy to a woman. They seemed an honest kindly people, happy in their homes and in their simple Buddhist faith and I doubt much if they had anything to gain from the introduction of European ideas. The Lushais and Shendus were made of different stuff and need very different dealing with".

At the time of the creation of a separate hill district in 1866, its headquarters were located at Chandrogona (the capital of Chakma Raja). Later on, in 1869, it was shifted by Superintendent Capt. Lewin to Rangamati with a view to paying the needed attention to the affairs of the front area which was then experiencing repeated raids on the British subjects by the Lushai tribes. In March 1863, the Superintendent of CHT Capt. Graham held a meeting with the Lushai Chiefs at Rothanpuia's village near south of Demagiri (likely the present location of Lungsen) and entered into an agreement with the Lushai Chiefs who, in return of payment in cash or kind agreed inter alia to acknowledge the authority of the government, prevent their clansmen from attacking British subjects or trading, cultivating or travelling on the hills and in case any dispute arising between them and the British subjects to refer it to the Superintendent for British subjects. But the results were not as expected and with the prevailing frontier situation, the British Government put pressure on the Chakma Chief to shift his capital from Chandrogona to Rangamati and ultimately it was shifted in 1874. The covenanted title of "Raja" was conferred on the Chakma Chief the same year.

After the expedition of 1872 in which Mary Winchester and other captives were surrendered to the Chittagong column, peace reigned for quite some years. However, in January 1888 three raids were made at different points of the frontier, the most serious being the massacre of Lieutenant Steward and the survey party of which he was in command. They were so near Rangamati that Lieutenant imagined that the party was secure from attack and, therefore, no precautious were taken to guard against the possibility of a surprise. All of a sudden a hunting party of Powis (Shendus) came charging on the unguarded encampment. They rushed and secured the heads of the party. Subsequently it transpired that Howsata, the Powi Chief, was in treaty to marry one of the princesses of Tlang tribe and a certain number of heads was demanded as a part of marriage portion. In the same month, a party of Haulong carried raids on the upper Chengri, killed thirty one people and took eight women into captivity. In 1890, military expeditions were launched simultaneously into the Chin Lushai Hill from Chittagong and Burma as the British Government was fully convinced that any plan for dealing with these hillsmen should be implemented in concert by the governments of Bengal, Assam and Burma and the captives were recovered. Again in 1892, the British Government sent columns to complete the punitive measures against these villagers who were mainly responsible for raids on the British subjects in the Chittagong hills and Cachar border.

Ultimately during 1895-96 the whole of the Kookie land was brought under the British control. In the course of operation against the Eastern Kookie (Lushai) in 1892, considerable difficulties had been experienced as a result of the diversion of administrative control over the Lushai country among the three authorities viz. Assam, Bengal and Burma. So after prolonged discussions it was finally decided to transfer the southern Lushai hills (a part of the then Chittagong Hill Tracts which had previously formed a part of Bengal) to Assam. Therefore the boundaries had to be re-demarcated.

The boundary of the hill tracts was originally demarcated by the British as below :

> "The Eastern boundary is formed by a line running from the South East of hill of Tippera along with the course of the Tuilenpui or Sajuk river to its junction with the Karnafulee and hence along the course of Tui-chang across the Uiphum range to the West and along the Thega Khal to its headwaters thence Westward along the watershed of the Wey bongtlang until it meets the southern hill station of Keokradong on the Arakan frontier. The administrative headquarters are at Rangamati."

On Ist April, 1900, the South and North Lushai hills were amalgamated to form a district of the Assam province and placed in charge of an officer styled as 'Superintendent of Lushai Hills" with headquarters at Aijal (now spelt Aizawl). The proclamation of the Government runs as follows :

> "Government of India No. 591-EB, whereas the territories known as the South Lushai hills, were by

a proclamation No. 1697-E, dated the 6th September 1895, issued under the Government of India Act 1865 (28 and 29 Vict., Cap. 17) section 4, included within the lower provinces of Bengal, and whereas the tract known as Ruttan Puya's villages, including Demagiri in the Hill Tracts of Chittagong is also included within the said lower provinces, and whereas it is expedient that the said territories and tract should now be placed under the administration of the Chief Commissioner of Assam ; known to all men, and it is hereby proclaimed, that the Governor-General in Council has been pleased, in exercise of the powers conferred by section 3 of the Government of India Act, 1854 (17 and 18 Vict., Cap. 77) and with the sanction and approbation of the Secretary of the State for India, to take the said territories and tract under his immediate authority and management, and to place them under the administration of the Chief Commissioner of Assam, and further to direct that henceforth they shall be included within the province of Assam."

Due to this revision of boundaries the Chakma Raja had to forego some of his lands as also the subjects who were inhabiting beyond the river Tega Khal.

With the passage of time the British Government realised that the constitution of hill district of 1860 would not work satisfactorily and consequently the regulation 1900 was adopted in place of earlier rules. The new regulation of the hill district of Chittagong came into force w.e.f. May 1900, making it out of bounds for the plain people (non-resident) and it is reproduced below :

Notification No. 123 PD, dated the Ist May : In exercise of the powers conferred on him by Section 18 of the Chittagong Hill Tracts Regulation, 1900, the Lieutenant Governor is pleased to lay down the following rules for the administration of these tracts :

1. The local Government may make rules for carrying into effect the objects and purposes of this regulation.

2. In particular and without prejudice to the generality to the foreign power, such rules may-

(a) Provide for the administration of civil justice in the Chittagong hill tracts ;

(b) Prohibit, restrict or regulate the appearance of legal practitioners in cases arising in the said tracts ;

(c) Provide for the registration of documents in the said tracts ;

(d) Regulate or restrict the transfer of land in the said tracts ;

(e) Provide for the Sub-Division of the said tracts into circles, those circles into Taluks and those Taluks into Mauzas.

(f) Provide for the collection of the rents and the administration of the revenue generally in the said circles, Taluks and Mauzas through the Chief Dewan and Headman ;

(g) Define the power and jurisdiction of the Chiefs, Dewans and Headmen and regulate the exercise by them of such power and jurisdiction ;

(h) Regulate the appointment and dismissal of Dewans and Headmen ;

(i) Provide for the remuneration of Chiefs, Dewans and Headmen and Village officers generally by the purpose or otherwise as may be thought desirable;

(j) Prohibit, restrict or regulate the migration and cultivation raiyats from one circle to another;

(k) Regulate the acquisition by Government of land required for public purposes;

(l) Provide for the levy of taxes in the said tracts; and,

(m) Regulate the procedure to be observed by officers acting under this regulation or the rules for the time being in force thereunder.

Till the advent of 1900 A.D., there was only one road known as the Chittagong-Demagiri-Lunglei-Haka road in this hill district. And this too was mainly a military track used for military expeditions in the frontier hill areas and for maintaining supply to the fort Lunglei and other advance military posts. The major part of the district consisted of wilderness. At thetime ofthe partition of Indian sub-continent in 1947 into two dominions of India and Pakistan, the Thega Khal stood as the common boundary for these two countries at this border. Therefore, the people on both sides of the international border Thega Khal came of the same ethnic stock i.e. the Chakmas. Until 1947, there was the predominance of the Buddhist population in the Chittagong Hill tracts, but in the following period this situation underwent a change. The break-up of the population of the Chittagong Hill Tracts (per ten thousand) on the basis of religion is given below:

Year	Buddhists	Hindus	Muslims	Others
1872	9718	85	197	–
1881	7287	1996	717	–
1891	7213	2345	442	–
1947	8505	1000	435	60
1980	5400	(–)	3861	739 (including Hindu population)

Thus from the above table it becomes clear that the number of Muslim population in the Chittagong Hill Tracts until the partition of the Indian sub-continent in 1947 was negligible and that the immigration of Muslim population was boosted only when this area was merged with Pakistan. As a consequence of this immigration the Chakms are being threatened to be reduced to the status of minority in their own home land and have been outnumbered by the outsider Muslims. They are a helpless spectator to this injustice and are unable to prevent the government backed influx of non-tribals into their home land.

The population of Chittagong Hill Tracts (in 000) from 1901 to 1981 is given as below:

District	1901	1911	1921	1931	1941	1951	1961	1971	1981
Chittagong Hill Tracts	125	154	173	213	247	288	385	508	746

Notes:

1. Chittagong Hill Tracks by R.H. Sneyd Hutchinson, p. 24.

2. History of the relation of the government with the hill tribes of North East Frontier of Bengal by Mackenzie.

3. The story of the Chakma Chief Raja Dharam Buksh Khan goes that the king once while wandering in the forest reached at a Jhum hut where he saw Kalabi, the only daughter of Gujang and was so much fascinated by Kalabi that he decided to make her his queen. The proposal of the king for her hand was accepted by Gujang Chakma. Latter she came to be known as Kallendi Rani and who by her sheer abilities earned for herself such a remarkable place in the Chakma history.

4. Chakma Jatir Itibritta by Biraj Mohan Dewan.

5. Kookie (Kuki)—From the earliest period of which we have any knowledge, the hills lying to the south of Manipur, Cachar and Sylhet (now in Bangladesh) have been inhabited by various tribes known to the Bengalees by the common name Kookie, Cookie, Kuki-North East Frontier of Bengal by Mackenzie.

6. Zo people and Kuki – When the British took possession of Bengal and had their contact with Zo people (the term

Mizo covers all Zo people) the Bengalees told them that Zo were Kuki – a Bengali word which means something like savage or wild hill people. But when the British came in close contact with Lusei they realised that they should not call them Kuki. Initially the British used the term 'LOOSYE', However, the British later adopted 'LUSHAI' as the official designation for ZO people–Zo History by Vumson.

7. Imperial Gazetteer of India, Vol.II, pp. 447–463.

CHAPTER 7

CHAKMAS AND THE PARTITION OF INDIA (1947)

On 16th August, 1947 came the declaration of Sir Cyrill Radcliffe, the Chairman of the Bengal Boundary Commission, for annexation of the Chittagong Hill Tracts (area: 5419 sq. miles; 98% of its population belonging to the Mongolian race and believing in Buddhism) with the sovereign Islamic nation of Pakistan which had been formed on 14th August, 1947 by the merger of the Muslim majority areas on the Eastern and Western Frontiers of undivided India. Some inhabitants of CHT, majority of them students, namely Ghansyam Dewan, Sneh Kumar Chakma, Lalit Mohan Chakma, Sroto Rajan Khisha, Rabindra Lal Chakma and others felt uneasy at the announcement of this annexation and rose in revolt against this declaration. A Chakma delegation headed by Kamini Mohan Dewan, a prominent Chakma leader, went to Delhi and avowed their allegiance to India.

The Muslim leaders of Pakistan, however, were quick to take the wind out of the Indian tricolour hoisted on many buildings in Rangamati and the Pakistan Government silenced the voice of dissent of these students with a heavy hand. Many Chakma students ran away from their home land CHT to evade harassment and atrocities at the hands of the government. Therefore, while the Buddhistic Mongoloid people of CHT were in deep resentment over their merger with Pakistan, the Pakistani authorities set about to transform CHT into a Muslim land as the very basis of the formation of Pakistan was religion—establishment of a separate home land for the Muslims in India.

The ethnic Mongoloid minority of the CHT was not provided opportunity of referendum to show their preference for merger either with India or Pakistan.The outcry of the tribal Buddhist people fell on the deaf ear of the authorities who were at that time busy shaping the future of the people of the Indian sub-continent. Thus the partition of India left the future of the oldest Buddhistic people of India under the (un) protective umbrella of the Muslims even though Buddhism originated in Hinduism and is still deemed a branch of Hinduism. Apparently the British did not take seriously the claim of the Buddhists that in their religion they were closer to the Hindus and not to the Muslims. Surprisingly this just and weighty claim of the tribal Buddhists did not cause much concern to the Hindu leaders either and as such no voice was raised by them against this arbitrary decision of annexation of CHT to Pakistan without providing any opportunity to its inhabitants to give their option.

As the luck favoured Pakistan, the Pakistani authorities lost no time in taking measures for integrating the ethnic Buddhist people of CHT with the majority Muslims in Pakistan lest it should go to India. The programmes of integration and drowning of the ethnic Buddhist groups in the Muslim majority were taken up simultaneously and those who stood up against the government policy were ruthlessly suppressed and as a result many had to cross border into India and Burma. With a view to further cementing this amalgamation the Pakistan Government conceived a scheme of setting up a hydro electric project on the river Karnafulee in CHT. This project was completed in 1960 and led to the inroads of Muslim population in CHT in large number; just what the government had contemplated about. The great influx of non-tribals into CHT took place under a well thought out policy of the government.

In the history of the last 300 years, the people of CHT have been successively dominated by different external powers. Their names and period of domination is given below:

Period	*Dominant power*
1660-1760	Muslim rulers (Mughals)
1760-1860	East India Company
1860-1947	British Monarch
1947 onwards	Muslim Rulers (Pakistanis and Bangladeshis)

In 1947, of the total population of the CHT the tribes-people and the Muslim Bengalis formed 98% and less than 2% respectively. The mainstay of the tribal population was Jhuming and the area was self-sufficient in agricultural produces, and rather enjoyed prosperity in food.

Now, together with the programme of settlement of Bengali Muslims, Government pursued the policy of establishing modern industries viz. paper mills hydroelectric projects and other ancillary industries at Chandroogona (CHT). These programmes created job opportunities for non-tribal population at the cost of the local tribal population. The high water level of Kaptai Hydro Electric Project inundated a vast Chakma inhabited area, which practically turned into a vast sheet of water uprooting many thousands families and in the absence of proper and adequate re-settlement programme many of them were forced to cross borders into the neighbouring countries namely India and Burma. The bulk of exodus numbering 40,000 took refuge in India in the province of North Eastern Frontier, now the State of Arunachal Pradesh. Similarly, over 20,000 people crossed over and settled down in the hills of Arakan bordering CHT in Burma. In the wake of these developments Muslim population in large number spilled over the hill tracts and swiftly outnumbered the ethnic Buddhist local tribes in a number of areas. The ethnic tribal inhabitants found themselves pushed into a desperate situation

They felt that a fist was directed against them, since the Pakistan Government was trying to circumvent the status of excluded area of CHT that had been granted to it by the British. Firstly, the term 'Tribal Area' was inserted in place of the term 'Excluded Areas' when the constitution of Pakistan was enacted. Following this the special status of CHT ceased from 1963. This resulted in the repealment of safeguards for the inhabitants of the tribal ethnic minorities in the CHT. Prior to the liberation of Bangladesh a kind of 'Matsyanyaya' (larger fish devouring the smaller one) had been prevailing in Pakistan. The tribals found themselves to be in a very sorry state.

The last general elections of united Pakistan were held in 1970 in which Chakma Rája Tridib Ray was elected to the parliament of Pakistan as an independent and Manabendra Narayan Larma was elected as an independent candidate to the Legislative Assembly of East Pakistan. Besides Bomong Chief Mong Chuge Prue Chawdhury was also elected to the Legislative Assembly as an Awami League candidate. The general elections results were in favour of Awami League (a political party of East Pakistan). Thereafter the political events in Pakistan gave new impetus to the demand of independence for East Pakistan and ultimately the Awami League made a declaration of independence on 25th March, 1971. A civil war broke out between the Bengali people of East Pakistan and Pakistan Government which ultimately ended in the defeat of Pakistan Government. The brutal repression of the people of Bangladesh by the Pakistan armed forces is now a well known fact of recent history. December 16,1971 was declared as a victory day and Bangladesh, the new name of East Pakistan, emerged as an independent sovereign state. Before the fall of East Pakistan Government, Chakma Raja Tridib Roy was whisked away to West Pakistan and has been living there since then without returning to his home land (CHT). That was the virtual end of the Buddhistic ruling line of the Chakma Kingship of CHT.

In 1972, a delegation consisting of 18 tribal leaders and headed by Manabendra Narayan Larma met the first President of Bangladesh Mujibur Rahman to discuss the demands of the tribal people of CHT which among others included the following :

(a) Autonomy for CHT with a legislature of its own.

(b) Retention of the Chittagong Hill Tracts Regulation of 1900 in the Bangladesh Constitution.

(c) Constitution of Tribal Chief's Office.

(d) Constitutional Provisions restricting the amendment of the 1900 regulation and imposition of a ban on influx of the non-tribal people into CHT.

The President rejected the demands of the Tribal leaders with scorn (it is said that the President angrily threatened to drown the tribals in a flood of people from plains) and the Tribal leaders had to return empty handed and greatly disillusioned.

In this atmosphere permeated with strong nationalistic feelings an underground political party under the banner of "Communist Party of Rangamati" took birth on 16th May, 1972 with the militant leaders in command and its overground nomenclature was "*JANA SAMHATI SMITI*" under the Chairmanship of Manabendra Narayan Larma. An armed wing was raised on 7th January, 1973, by Jana Samhati Samiti under the banner "*SHANTI BAHINI* (*PEACE FORCE*)".

The new Bangladesh Government likewise continued to follow the policy which it inherited from the previous Government i.e. to equate and amalgamate the Mongolian ethnic races of Buddhist faith with the Bangali race. The mental agony of Mongolian races was on the increase as no solution of their problem was in sight for so long. The Chakma leaders refused to accept the Bangladesh constitution of 1972.

The first general elections in Bangladesh were held in 1973 in which Manabendra Narayan Larma and Chaitoai Rouza were elected to the Parliament from CHT and they demanded for regional autonomy in the Bangladesh Parliament. The political events following the general elections put the Bangladesh Government off the rails. As a result the, Government banned all political parties and made a one party Government. Ultimately, the military authorities took over from the civilian

Government through a military coup. Manabendra Narayan Larma went underground as the military Government became very suspicious of him. However, his brother Jyotirindra Narayan Larma (Santu), an active member of Shanti Bahini, was arrested.

In 1975, a second delegation consisting of 67 representatives of all cross section of tribal population of hill tracts met the President, Justice A.S Sayam of Bangladesh to put forward their demand but all to no end. Likewise in 1976, similar proposals were presented to the new President of Bangladesh, Military General Ziaur Rahman (in 1975, military took over the power from the civilian Government). The military regime instead of showing sympathy adopted a hard line towards the problem of the Buddhist minority. It was decided to solve the problems of the Buddhist minority tribe of CHT by military way. In pursuance of this line the Bangladesh army and para military forces were on the trail of Shanti Bhaini. The large scale Bengali Muslim population movement was followed in more vigorous and gigantic manner by the military Government. The Bengali Muslim peasantry in massive strength, numbering 50,000, were brought in and provided with liberal doles and got settled in CHT. The confidence of the tribal people was badly shaken when it became evidently clear that their country would not remain theirs for long and many of them migrated into neighbouring states to live with their brethren who had earlier crossed over into India and Burma. The CHT was swamped over by the military and para military forces whose numbers were as follows :

	Combat force	*Unit*
1.	Bangladesh Army	80,000 Men
2.	Bangladesh Rifles	25,000 ,,
3.	Ansara (Islamic guards)	5,000 ,,
4.	Armed Police	10,000 ,,
5.	Combatant Force at Guerrilla training centre	1,800 ,,
	Total :	1,21,800 Men

This military deployment in the district caused panic and fear among the inhabitants of the hill district and they were on the edge. The Bengali Muslim peasantry backed by Army occupied the land of the tribal inhabitants. It appalled the minority ethnic tribal group. With a view to assuaging the wounded feelings of the Tribals the military Government formed a tribal convention in 1977, but it failed to yield any result as the people considered it a wolf in sheep's clothing. Against this backdrop the Jana Samhati Samiti reviewed their programmes and policies in their second party congress which was held in the underground headquarters near Rangamati in Bangladesh. After this, heavy military operations were undertaken and Government troops carried out great massacres. The Anti-Slavery Society and other international human right organisations charged the Bangladesh Government that tribals in the CHT were being subjected to an ongoing Government backed campaign of murder, rape, eviction and sometimes forcible conversion to Islam !

In 1979, general elections took place in Bangladesh and Upendra Lal Chakma supported by Jana Samhati Samiti was elected as member to the Bangladesh parliament. Bangladesh Government constituted a tribal convention (Liaison Committee) with a view to initiating negotiations with the rebel Chakmas but without any success. In reality the Liaison Committee never occupied itself in doing anything and was on the wane gradually as happened earlier in the case of Tribal convention. The Government continued anti insurgency campaign and tried to woo people by making dispensations. Jyotirindra Narayan Larma (also known as Santu) was released from jail custody in the year 1980, but later again joined the underground movement. However, Dhaka Government took a firm decision to give full powers to military to do away with insurgency movement and the military forces came into play which resulted in Kalampali massacre where many houses were burnt and properties looted. The villagers were rounded up and divided into groups, the men and elderly women were shot at. The girls and young women were raped, Buddhist monks were tortured and many of them were killed. As a result many Chakmas fled to the forests in Indian state. In the month of December (1980) Bangladesh government tried to introduce a bill of disturbed area act for Chittagong hill tracts but it was violently opposed by the opposition party members in the parliament and it had to be withdrawn and was not moved again. The Dhaka Government was under pressure to end the war against the Chakma rebels, but no negotiations were initiated for a peaceful solution of the Buddhist ethnic tribes. Meanwhile there was a military coup in Bangladesh following which Lieutenant General Hussain Mohammad Ershad came to power.

Dhaka Government received reports of carnages by the Shanti Bahini and its raids on the new settlers at Bhusansara area of Barkal Upa Zilla in which at least 80 people were killed and many were seriously injured. A reign of terror was unleashed in many settlement areas by Shanti Bahini. Indian Government had to seal the border along the Bangladesh border in Mizoram and Tripura States by deputing large number of troops of Indian Border Security Force (BSF) and Central Reserve Police Force (CRPF).

The year 1982 turned out to be a very crucial and darkened year for Jana Shamhati Samiti, since many in the rank and file of Shanti Bahini became disillusioned and despaired with the leadership in the party. There was an upheaval in the party which resulted in a vertical division in the party in the 3rd general congress session of the Jana Samhati Samiti.

This critical issue sparked off an internal conflict among the upper echelons of leadership, and ultimately in an armed clash on June 14, 1983 between two factions of insurgents in the Chittagong hills. Thirty members of the outlawed Shanti Bahini were killed including their leader Manabendra Narayan Larma and more than 22 injured. Thereafter, one faction which was faithful to Manabendra Narayan Larma, was led by his younger brother Jyotirindra Narayan Larma and the other faction was headed by Priti Kumar Chakma.

The Larma group is commonly known as "Lamba" (long) and the Priti group is known as "Badi" (Short).

Taking advantage of this internal conflict in Shanti Bahini, Bangladesh government proclaimed a general amnesty on 3rd October, 1983 and also wanted to turn the situation to the advantage of the government by announcing encouraging proposals for years. Bangladesh governmert also assured that those rebels who had been convicted or facing trial would be released and job opportunities would be created for them. But all these proposals failed to allure the rebels who sent an open letter reply to the President of Bangladesh.

On 10th November, 1983, American and Dutch experts of Shell petroleum company who were engaged in dredging work in Kachalang area were taken as captives by the Larma faction of Shanti Bahini. The captives were released only after 49 days and after paying a handsome ransom of one and half crore of rupees and 19 kgs of gold. From the events that followed after the killing of Manabendra Narayan Larma, it was seen that the Larma Group was as vibrant as before, However, attempts were taken towards the unity of the two factions but it failed to bridge up the differences.

After the killing of Manabendra Narayan Larma, Shanti Bahini ran into difficulties and jeopardised the chances of controlling the lever in the organisation. A sense of despair and mistrust developed among the rank and file in both the groups. Taking advantage of this situation, Bangladesh security forces launched attacks on the hideouts of Shanti Bahini at various places namely Naraichari and Khagarachari areas. Bangladesh Security Forces also seized a huge quantity of ammunition during these operations. Dhaka Government believed that the strength of Shanti Bahini began to ebb and with a view to assuaging the tribal feelings appointed Upendra Lal Chakma (Ex-member of Parliament of Bangladesh) as adviser to the President of Bangladesh on tribals affairs with the status of a Minister. On 29th April, 1985, just one day before the closing date of amnesty offer as announced by the Government of Bengladesh, 233 Shanti Bahini insurgents capitulated to the Government authority. The bulk of surrenderers came from Priti Kumar group but the majority of Larma faction endured with arms.

The military President Lt. Gen. Hussain Muhammad Ershad, right from he beginning of the year 1985 made enticements of return of democracy, but people doubted the President's plea as it being a wolf in sheep's clothing. In the first quarter of the following year 1986, however, military Government made an announcement of general elections on the basis of adult franchise to be held on 7th March, 1986. This was the country's third general election. In the election arena there were two main political parties; one Bangladesh President Lt. Gen. H.M. Ershad's Jatiya Party and the other Awami League led by Sheikh Hasina, daughter of assassinated Ist President of Bangladesh Sheikh Mujibur Rahman. The numbers of new Bengali Muslim settlers who proliferated rapidly in Chittagong hill Tracts stood as the backbone of Ershad's Jatiya party but for the Tribals it was a no gain situation since the ethnic issue was still hanging in balance and they aimed to make a side-line with Awami party. Thereby the belligerent feelings between the Tribals and the Bengali Muslims in the hill tracts once again reached the culmination point during the election campaign.

Bangladesh authorities reported that in a series of incidents the Chakma insurgents killed 30 people including 8 Bangladesh security personnel and about 18 Muslim resettlers who were earlier rehabilitated in the hill tracts by the Dhaka authorities; reports from other side claim that election carnage took the life of 300 tribals. To stop the Shanti Bahini attacks on Government forces, retaliatory military operations were launched against the tribals leaving heap of dead bodies in villages and which eventually resulted in influx of tribal refugees into Tripura and Mizoram States of India. By the end of June 1986, about 19,000 refugees entered into Demagiri area in South Mizoram but this group was pushed back as reported in a local newspaper 'Hilander' in Mizoram in its issue dated 23rd June, 1986. Eventually Govt. of India assumed full resposibility for the expenditures on the refugees in Tripura.

When the situation had become extremely grave, the Bangladesh Government announed a month long amnesty for Shanti Bahini guerrillas making it valid till 25th June, 1986. General Ershad urged the insurgents to give up arms and surrender to authorities promising an economic settlement after the surrender. As reported in the daily Statesman in its issue dated 28th May, 1986, "The Tribals suspect an ominous design in some of the development activities which are being financed by western agencies. A 129 crore Bangladesh Taka project has already been initiated with funds from Australia for the construction of 13 new roads covering a total length of 343 miles to link up the inaccessible regions with the mainstream."

A multinational oil company has already announced its decision to spend a huge amount in the area during the next 25 years for exploring oil and natural gas in the rea. This is the highest amount to be spent on a single project in the area. A British agency is also providing money for developing Dhaka's telecommunication link with the interior.

It has also been alleged that experts belonging to a western defence ageney specially equipped for counter-insurgency extended help to Dhaka authorities in drawing up the security reorganisation plan for the hill tracts. Government of India has taken over the issue with the Bangladesh Government to take back the tribal refugees at various official and political level discussions, but it failed to resolve the issue. The refugees declined to return till a favourable condition returned in their home land. While these talks were being held the number of refugees continued to swell in Tripura. By March 1987, more than 50 thousand Buddhist tribals crossed over to Tripura from Bangladesh. This influx of tribals is considered the worst since June 1964, when over 52,000 Tribal Buddhist migrated into India from their ancestral home land CHT, in the erstwhile East Pakistan following inundation of their green patches of their valley by impounded water of Kaptai Hydro Electric project on the river Karnafulee.

Impartial observers like Amnesty International expressed 'grave concern' over the gross violation of human rights in CHT in its special report issued in Holland in June 1986. The Sunday magazine in one of its issue in March 1987 reported that "The 13000 sq. km. stretch of CHT in Bangladesh has become the rendezvous of Pakistani agents, Sikh terrorists and anti Indian rebel group". The said magazine also reported that "The former American national security adviser Zbigniew Brzenzski had described the CHT region as 'the beginning of the area of instability of South- East Asia'. Recently the attention of the U.N. has been drawn by Norway on the withering away of human rights in CHT.

Parbatya Chattagram Jana Samhati brought out on 29th January, 1987, a list of 689 cases of genocide and atrocities committed by Bangladesh forces and Bengali Muslim peasantry settlers in CHT from November 1986 to 19th January, 1987.

Therefore, an extraordinary state of affairs is prevailing in Chittagong hill tracts and the history of the ethnic Buddhist inhabitants therein is the history of constant war for ethnic survival, and history alone shall finally decide the fate of the last remnants of the oldest Buddhist culture and civilization whether they would survive or not.

CHAPTER 8

CHAKMAS IN INDIA :MIZORAM

The western part of Mizoram bordering Bangladesh is inhabited by the Chakmas. Dr. Mrs. N. Chatterjee in her book '*PUAN THE PRIDE OF MIZORAM*' noted that it is an irony of fate that Chakmas of Mizoram have at present sunk to utter degeneration even though they were, in not very distant past, the proud possessors of a distinctly developed culture. The corner-stone of this culture was based on the principle of plain living and high thinking. The British hegemony sprang up in Lushai Hills (now Mizoram) through this region of Chakma inhabited areas. A border town on the bank of river Karnafulee, Demagiri, in Mizoram still retains the traces of the ancient history of the earlier settlers. The word Demagiri is an Indo-Arakanese word, signifying the following: De-Deb-Debta-God (Sanskrit/Pali word, Ma—people or nation (Arakanese word) and Giri—mountain (Sanskrit/Pali word). Therefore, Demagiri means an abode of god (Men). The original people of this place must have been the admixture of Indo-Arakanese culture as the name suggests. After the formation of the Union Territory of Mizoram, the Mizoram

Assembly passed a bill to change the original name of the place from Demagiri to Tlabung (a Mizo name).

North Arakan, Chittagong Hill Tracts, Western part of Mizoram and Tripura are knitted together with network of rivers. All these river routes and valleys are dotted with Chakma villages. These bordering strategic tracts are dominated by the Chakmas. As explained earlier, a group of Chakmas beyond the river Thega i.e. western bank of the river fled to Lushai hills (now Mizoram) when this part was separated from Bengal and made a district of Assam province during the British period. This area inhabited by the Chakmas became part of Mizoram in India after the partition of Indian sub-continent in 1947.

After the independence of India, the Constituent Assembly of India became concerned with the administration of the backward regions of Assam inhabited by the Mongolian clan of Tibeto-Burman race. The Constituent Assembly, therefore, added the Sixth Schedule to the Constitution of India. The origin of this Schedule, in fact, can be traced back to the British period when the British Government passed Act X in 1822 for the governance of the people of the Tibeto-Burman races in the hill tracts in India. This act was amended from time to time according to the need of the time and amendments were effected by the Indian Council Acts of 1861, 1869 and 1874. The Governor-General identified the following territories in the province of Assam as the most backward tracts :—

1. The Garo hills Districts;
2. The British portion of Khasi and Jaintia hill district, other than Shillong Municipality and Cantonment;
3. The Mikir Hills (in Nowgong and Sibsagar district);
4. The north Cachar hills (in Cachar district);
5. The Naga hill district;
6. The Lushai hills district;
7. The Sadiya Frontier Tracts;
8. The Lakhimpur Frontier Tracts.

Subsequently, for the above reasons the area came to be known as Tribal areas of Assam for the administration of which the Sixth Schedule was enactcd and passed into law.

According to the provision of this Sixth Schedule the Lushai hill (a district of Assam) turned to be an autonomous district under a dual administration of Government and District Council. In 1954, by an Act of parliament the name of the Lushai hill district was changed to Mizo Hill District under the Sixth Schedule and some powers of the state Government were delegated to the Autonomous District Council body for manning the affairs of the districts. 1952 was a very historic year, during which Autonomous District Council came into being and was granted legislative, exeecutive and judicial powers. The management and control of the following subjects were vested in the District Council: (1) Allotment of lands, (2) Forests, (3) Primary education, (4) Establishment of VIllage Administration, (5) Inheritance of Property, (6) Marriage and Social customs. The District Councial was also empowered to levy taxes on profession, trade and employment.

In 1953, a Regional Council (Pawi-Lakher) was also set up in the South of Mizo District where the hill tribals namely Pawi, Lakhers and Chakmas are in majority. The Regional Council was vested with similar powers within its jurisdiction, excepting that it did not have control over primary education. The Chakma population was represented in both the Councils. (2/3rds of the total Chakma population in the District Council and the remaining 1 /3rd in the Regional Council.) They could comfortably consolidate their votes in promoting Chakma members in both the Councils.

During the period 1952-71, under the dual rule of Assam Government and the Autonomous District Council the Mizo Hill District (now Mizoram) had undergone great transformation and the Mizo people became wedded deeply to the concept of the rule of law and democracy. But their journey all these years was not all that pleasant as the nature failed to produce enough food for their subsistence. The cry for food echoed from one hill to another. Timely help was hindered in the absence of communication and administrative infrastructure. People were hard hit by the famine and on 1st March, 1966, there was a general revolt against the Govt. of India under the banner of Mizo National Front (which was earlier known as Mizo Famine Front) under the leadership of Mr. Laldenga. So the people harboured much bitterness against the government, since the rebellion is not a parlour game. Of course the Central Government was equally desirous of winn-ing over the hearts of the Mizo people. It was a no-win-no-loss situation for the government.

The Government of India ultimately decided to upgrade the status of the Mizo hill district to the status of Union Territory as one of the wings of Central Government. Accordingly, the Mizo district Council came to be abolished in accordance with the North Eastern Area Act of 1971, and in its place a new Union Territory of *MIZORAM* came into being in 1972. Thus a new chapter for the minorities of Mizoram was opened from 2nd April, 1972, with the setting up of three district councils, out of the defunct Pawi-Lakher Council. These are as follows:

1. The Chakma District Council;
2. The Pawi District Council;
3. The Lakher District Council.

In 1972, the Head Quarters of the Chakma District Council were first located at Borapansury, on the river bank of Thega (an international river boundary between India and Bangladesh in the western border of Mizoram). The persons who manned the Council in the beginning were nominated by the Government from all strata of the Chakma. Their names are given below:

1. Atul Chandra Chakma (I);
2. Arun Kumar Dewan;
3. Gunadhar Chakma;
4. Majur Dhaj Chakma;
5. Satya Chakma;
6. Ananda Kumar Chakma.

As a rule the executive functions of the Council is vested in the Chief Executive member who is elected by the members from amongst themselves. The chair of the Chief Executive member for the first time was held by Atul Chandra (I), while Majurdhaj Chakma was made its first Chairman and both of them held their respective posts till 10th October, 1972. The first election for the Chakma District Council came at the end of the year 1972, and 8 members were elected on the basis of adult franchise. The first batch of the elected representatives in the Council consisted of the following:

1. Nilomoni Chakma;
2. Atul Chandra Chakma (II);
3. Sneha Kumar Chakma;
4. Chitra Mohan Chakma;
5. Ganga Chakma;
6. Laichoka Tongchhunga;
7. Malkhan Chandra Riang;
8. Rotliangha.

Bhrigumoni Chakma was included in the Council as nominated member and with this the total members of the Council rose up to 9. Chitra Mohan Chakma was seated to the chair of the Chairman of the District Council, and Nilomoni Chakma was elected by the Council in session as its first Chief Executive Member. The Executive Committee was constituted with Sneha Kumar Chakma and Laichoka Tongchhunga.

The members of the Council, however, soon developed acute differences of opinion among themselves and within a year's time it resulted in the tabling of no-confidence motion against the Chief Executive member. The said motion was tabled on 29th January, 1974 and the following day i.e on 30th January, 1974 the Council in session elected Sneh Kumar Chakma to the Chair of the Chief Executive member and the Executive Committee was reconstituted with the following members:

1. Malkhan Chandra Rai;
2. Rotlingha.

The foremost task before the executive committee was the shifting of Head Quarters of the Council from Borapansury to Chengkawrlui (a Mizo name now Kamalanagar) for the reason that Borapansory was on the international broder and eventually the Council office was shifted to the new location. The selection of site at Borapansury was an utter mistake as viewed by some of the members. The struggle, however, for search of a better site for the Head Quarters of the Chakma District Council is not over as yet, as some Chakma leaders feel that the present location suffers from insurmountable geographical disadvantages which alienates development programmes. Soon afterwards the Chairman Chitra Mohan Chakma vacated his seat by submitting his resignation w.e.f. 18 April, 1975 (the reason of resignation was not let out). The Council in session on 12th May, 1975 elected Nilomoni Chakma to the Chair of the Chairman. The Council by and by became a byword of mismanagement and finally government appointed a one man Commission vide Government notification No. LAD/A-23/73/170 dated 15 November 75 to enquire as to whether the administration of the District Council was carried on in accordance with the provisions of the Sixth Schedule of the Constitution of India.

The Commission duly completed its enquiry into the various allegations and in its report it was pointed out that the administration in the District Council neglected the observance of the financial rules and regulations and official procedures and had failed to carry on the administration in confirmity with the provisions of the Sixth Schedule of the constitution.

On the basis of the report of the Enquiry Commission, the Executive Committee of the Council was dissolved w.e.f. 15th October, 1976 (forenoon) and the Lieutenant Governor (administrator) resumed the executive, financial and administrative function vide Government notification No. LAD/A-9/76/45 the 27th September, 1976. The Legislative power of the Council was, however, retained. The Council remained under suspension from 15.10.76 to 32-1-78. On 12th December, 1977 a general election was held to end the administrator's period and the newly elected representatives of the Council were as follows :

1. Nilomoni Chakma;
2. Sukromoni Chakma;
3. Kalapho Tongchhunga;
4. Ganga Chakma (died on 9.11.79);
5. Bijita Nanda Dewan;
6. Chitra Kumar Chakma;
7. Tawnenga;
8. V.Saplina.

Jalak Kumar Tongchhunga was nominated by the Government as member of the Council. Ganga was elected to the chair of the Chairman and the Council in session on 15th March 1978 elected Nilomoni Chakma as the new Chief Executive member. Bijita Nanda Dewan and Chitra Kumar Chakma were included in the Executive Committee w.e.f. 18th March 1978.

The Executive Committee, however, could not get along for long and therefore, it was reshuffled on 16th January, 1979. The new executive members were Sukramoni Chakma and Kalapho Tongchhunga. The chairman Ganga Chakma breathed his last on 9th November 1979 and in the resultant vacancy Mahabab Chakma was elected in the byelection. They succeeded in pulling together and ruling the Council for the full term.

On 4th September, 1981, an emergency session was held wherein the district council unanimously decided to shift back the Head Quarters of the Chakma District Council from Kamalanagar to Borapansury, but the Government declined to approve it on administrative grounds. At the expiration of the tenure of the elected members, the 3rd general election of the Council was held in the month of December 1982, as a result of which the following persons were elected:

1. Pulin Bayan Chakma;
2. Atul Chandra Chakma (II);
3. Nutan Kumar Chakma;
4. Jalak Kumar Chakma;
5. Birash Mohan Chakma;
6. Susen Chakma;
7. Punya Chakma;
8. Arun Bikash Chakma;
9. Adikanta Tongchhungya;
10. Ramoni Chakma.

(Due to the increase in the number of constituencies the total number of elected representatives was raised from 9 to 10.)

Dayal Dhan Chakma was nominated by the Government as a member of the Chakma District Council. Nutan Kumar Chakma was seated to the chair of the Chairman on 24th January, 1983. The Council in session on 27th January, 1983 elected Romani Chakma as new Chief Executive member. Punya Chakma and Birash Mohan Chakma were included in the executive committee. The executive committee, however, lasted for a very short period and on 18th April, 1983 during the first sitting of the Council a no-confidence motion was tabled by Atul Chandra Chakma (II) and it was admitted. Therefore, the Council in session on 21st April, 1983 elected Pulin Bayan Chakma, the new Chief Executive Member. The executive committee was reshuffled with the inclusion of new members Atul Chandra Chakma and Jalak Kumar Tongchhungya.

Atul Chandra Chakma (II), however, submitted his resignation soon after and it was accepted in July 1984 by the Lieutenant Governor. Soon there was a discovery regarding some irregularities in the distribution of Council funds and the members were much agitated over this discovery. The disgruntled members which formed the majority stood against the CEM in the the Council session held in December 1986 and subsequently elected Nutan Kumar Chakma as CEM. But this election did not receive the approval of the Government till 30th March, 1987 (the delay as learnt was due to Government's preoccupation with the general election of the new State of Mizoram).

The disgruntled members also brought a no-confidence motion against the Chairman and Government authorised the Council in session to elect a new Chairman and accordingly Dayal Dhan Chakma was elected as new Chairman in the month of April 1987.

Shortly after the conclusion of first general election in the new state of Mizoram in February 1987, some Chakma leaders formed a nationalistic front by the name of "*CHAKMA JATIYA PARISHAD*" which was affiliated to the *MIZO NATIONAL FRONT*, the ruling political party in the State. The majority of the leaders in the CDC had resigned from Congress and joined the newly formed party to turn over a new leaf. The term of the present elected members ends in 1987.

The Chakma District Council solely depends on the central fund which is given in the shape of grant-in-aid through the state Government. The jurisdiction of the CDC covers five subjects over which it exercises power viz. (1) Forest, (2) Water Supply, (3) Rural Communication, (4) Primary Education and (5) Sanitation.

This endowment fund to the District Council is provided under the head of "Essential Services" of the State Government. The state Government has also been providing a dole to the Council.

Over the last 14 years of the existence of the Chakma District Council the life in the rural area under its jurisdiction registered improvement in the following limited spheres:

(i) Primary Education

The education at the primary level is a joint responsibility of the CDC and the state Government; policy matters and financial control in the hands of the education department while general management and supervision lies with the CDC. The education above the primary level in the Council area is controlled exclusively by the state Government. As per the available information no full-hearted education programmes are followed in the Bengali Medium Chakma Schools nor are these schools receiving guidance in such matters as text books, framing of curricular and the examination system.

As a result though the number of students has increased over the years, the quality of education in these schools is far below standard. Nothing will cure it unless Government takes over these sub-standard schools. The figures given below show the progress in the establishment of schools in Chakma District Council area:

Sl. No.	Schools	Total No. as in 1972	Total No. as in 1983
1.	Primary School	7	63
2.	Middle School	Nil	3
3.	High School	Nil	Nil

There are also Bengali medium Primary and Middle Schools for Chakma students outside the jurisdiction of the Chakma District Council. These schools are under the direct control of the education department of the state Government.

The literacy rate among the Chakmas is very low; among men it is 20% and among women 7% which is much lower than the literacy rate in Mizoram as a whole which is as high as 60%. What is to be held responsible for this educational retardation of the Chakmas is their strong belief in the study of Bengali in the face of a general antipathy in the whole of the North Eastern Zone against the domination of the Bengali ethnic race and their language. This shows that the Chakmas are riding a wrong horse which may ultimately push them into serious troubles as regards their over-all development.

(ii) Administration of Social Justice

Over a decade has passed, since the Chakma District Council came into existence, but not a single case of social dispute was brought to the district council for discussion or adjudication. Why so ? Is it because the District Council is unable to exercise its judicial power or the people are most peace loving or the people do not repose full faith in the judicial court of the District Council? The reasons are yet to be ascertained. It is an imperative need that the powers of the District Council are made effective without further delay. The North Eastern Council, Shillong has sponsored a programme through Law Research Institute, Eastern Region (Gauhati High Court) of codifying the customary laws of the Chakmas. As it is seen now, in the absence of proper codification of social and customary laws, the courts of the District Council are rendered infructuous. Therefore, the district council has been an autonomous body without having any set up of rules of its own for its management and functioning.

(iii) Sanitation and Water Supply

1981-91 has been declared the International Decade of drinking water supply and sanitation to provide every citizen with safe drinking water. Availability of drinking water supply in the villages is one of the major objectives to be achieved in this international decade. Therefore, it would be most befitting to look at the progress in achieving these objectives in the villages of the Chakma District Council. The total number of villages in the Council, comprising small and big villages, comes to 40.

The water of rivers Tuichong and Thega is the main source of water supply for majority of the villages in the Chakma District Council. A few villages also depend on the streams and perennial water sources. The water obtained from these sources is not suitable for drinking purpose. The waters of Thega and Tuichong are the most unhygienic as these are slow moving and get polluted by the disposal of waste material by the inhabitants of the river banks into these rivers. Therefore, the District Council is provided funds on year to year basis to be spent on sanitation and water supply schemes. During 1972-83 as high an amount as Rs.10 lakhs was made available for this purpose. If the figures of total expenditure incurred on these schemes are to be recounted, they will tell a tale of steady progress.

(iv) Forest

Despite the fact teat the whole of the Chakma District Council area constitutes a forest area, the Council is given regular grant for raising forest of specific categories. The fact being that there were no profitable forest resources in the whole of the district Council area, since no afforestation programmes were undertaken here for raising profitable species since earliest period.

(v) Rural Communication

All schemes of maintenance of intra village path, foot track between the villages are executed through the District Council. In such rural schemes, majority of the villagers participate which in a way give them a lever to raise their earnings. It is also otherwise a community work or people's task. The expenditure on this has increased manifold in recent years as compared to a decade back. In rural areas this has formed as a traditional work system. Therefore, there is a visible mark of quick progress in rural communication in the Council area and very soon the area will be tied with the net work of roads.

Conclusion

To conclude this discussion of the Chakma District Council, I would like to speak first of all about the people for whom this Council was brought into being. A role has been assigned to the people of remote hill areas in the welfare programmes undertaken by various Central and State Government agencies. The society in the Council area is comparatively small and less complex and the people, therefore, can find a meaningful role for themselves in the activities of the Council.

By and large, the performance of the Council over the years has not been very satisfactory and it has rather become a byword of mismanagement. An in-depth study of the functioning of Council reveals that it has faced substantial hurdles due to lack of an administrative infrastructure, effective control and other supporting factors. In any pioneering effort such hurdles are bound to come. Efforts, however, should continue for bringing about the desired improvement by laying the necessary administrative infrastructure and strengthening the system. The task may be difficult but certainly not impossible to accomplish given the strong desire of the government to better the lot of Chakmas in every sphere.

CHAPTER 9

ROLE OF THE CHAKMAS IN MIZORAM POLITICS

The first ever election to the Mizoram General Assembly was held on the basis of adult franchise in the first quarter of 1972 i.e. soon after the attainment of status of Mizoram Union Territory from Mizo District Council as a part of Assam. The Mizoram Union Territory had a unicameral legislature consisting of 33 members—30 elected and 3 nominated. This electoral battle was fought between the two dominant political parties namely Mizo Union (the earstwhile ruling party in the District Council) and the National Congress (Although there were also other political parties in the fray but they were of little importance). The election results came as a great shock to the Congress party as it suffered an utter rout. Out of total 30 Assembly seats for which the elections were held Mizo Union secured 24 seats while Congress could win only 6 seats. Out of which Chakmas won two seats—one by Hari Kristo Chakma from Demagiri Constituency and the other by Satya Priya Chakma from Chawngte Constituency, where the majority of the voters were Chakmas, and whose allegiance to the Congress was a well known fact.

They had been loyal to Congress from the time of beginning of insurgency in Mizoram in March 1966, when the Mizo National Front (originally formed in 1959 as Mizo Famine Front which later changed into a political party *MIZO NATIONAL FRONT* led by Laldenga gave a call for the establishment of sovereign independent Mizoram. But soon after the eruption of insurgency this political party was banned by the Govt. of India.

The traditional system of administration of Lushai Hills (now Mizoram) by the Lushai Chiefs ceased with the setting up of Mizo District Council after the independence of India. The move for the establishment of democratic system of administration was spearheaded by the Mizo Union. The political ideology of this political party appealed a great deal to the masses. Therefore, it championed for the ushering in of a democratic system in Mizo society. The two dominant political parties namely Mizo National Front and Mizo Union developed sharp differences in the early sixties when Mizo National Front propounded the theory of a sovereign independent Mizoram. At that time, the National Congress had not gained much influence in Mizo District and was functioning under the wing of Assam Pradesh Congress. With the attainment of the status of Union Territory of Mizoram, the District Congress was elevated to the status of Mizoram Pradesh Congress and was separated from Assam Pradesh Congress. This was the contextual political scenario in which Mizoram woke up to a new dawn for establishing a Government in the new born Union Territory. The first ever Government of Union Territory of Mizoram was formed by the political party 'Mizo Union' as stated before and it took office in May 1972 but the Mizoram ministry was under pressure from both Congress and MNF and came to an abrupt end following the murder of the Inspector General the Deputy Inspector General and Superintendent of Police at Police Head Quarters at Aizawl in 1975. The Ministry thus lasted two years only. Later on, the merger of Mizo Union with Congress took place as a result of which a Congress Government assumed office in Mizoram in 1974. The Congress Ministry was expanded and it was composed as follows: Chief Minister, 4 Ministers of Cabinet rank and two Deputy Ministers. The Ministry completed its 5 year term and on the completion of the term, Mizoram was brought under President's Rule. The President's Rule which lasted a year was imposed with view to activating operation against the MNF (underground Organisation which had virtually paralysed the functioning of Government Offices at the Capital Aizawl. The intense firing of MNF held up the capital town. It was true that the Government was confronted with an uphill task and the security forces geared up operations against MNF . The public in general were against putting the screw over the MNF. At the end of 1974, a retired Brigadier of Indian Army, Thenphunga Sailo founded a Human Right Committee at an opportune time and took up the cases of atrocities of security forces with the highest authorities. Brigadier Sailo explained that "The Human Right Committee wish that the public in India should be taken into confidence so that they should know the true state of affairs in Mizoram". This slogan of Brigadier Sailo held the public spell bound for a long time and later this Human Right Committee turned into a political party called People's Conference in April 1975. Brigadier Sailo emerged as a big political force in Mizoram and his party won Parliamentary seat in Mizoram in March 1977 elections. After the completion of one year of President's rule in Mizoram, the Election Commission of India held elections for Mizoram Legislative Assembly in 1978, which was fought by People's Conference, Congrees (I) and Mizoram Janata Party and other political parties. The election results came as a great setback to the Congress party. The number of seats won by different political parties was as follows :

1.	People's Conference	23
2.	Congress (I)	4
3.	Mizoram Janata	1
4.	Independent	2
	Total :	30

Out of 4 Congress candidates elected, Hari Kriste Chakma was elected from Demagiri Constituency (a Congress stronghold) and the other three were from Mizo communities. Kristo Mohan Chakma was elected as an independent candidate from Chawngte constituency. The People's Conference Ministry took office in June 1978, but after 5 months President's rule was re-imposed due to floor-crossing by some ruling party M.L.As. There was a vertical split in the People's Conference, one faction was led by Brigadier T. Sailo and the other by Thangradima and others. The third General Assembly elections were held in the month of April 1979 and the results of the election are as follows :

1.	People's Conference	21
2.	Congress (I)	8
3.	Independent	1
	Total :	30

Therefore, the People's Conference was back into power after six months and this time it completed its full 5 year term i.e upto April 1984.

Hari Kriste Chakma, one of the Congress (I) MLAs, was elected from Demagiri Constituency. However, the other Chakma MLA Sneha Kumar Chakma was elected from Chawngte Constituency as an independent. Later Sneha Kumar Chakma supported People's Conference, the ruling party, being aware of the fact that one cannot make omelette without breaking eggs. In the above context the 4th General Assembly elections were very crucial for all the political parties especially so for People's Conference and Congress (I) as it signified that the people of Mizoram were by the side of the regional parties. The minority Chakmas were deeply attached to Congress in their psyche sinc long, but their faith in the national party was shaken in the wake of rise of regional political parties. The results of the 2nd and 3rd General Assembly Elections would clearly justify the fact that the Chakmas had deviated from their traditional allegiance to Congress. The Chakmas were seriously considering to keep up with the times and to step out of their old conviction in the Congress (I) party but since no regional party had made any base in Chakma areas and there was also no prospect of any regional party of consolidating their position in that area so they had no alternative. In April 1983, in the by-election of Phuldungsei Constituency (following the killing of the PC MLA by some unknown assailants) the Chakmas stuck to their traditional belief and caused success of the Congress (I) candidate as against People's Conference candidate. The result of this by-election caused a concern to the minorities But the confidence of the minority peoples in the Regional parties waned when they found that some regional groups (political parties) were demanding deletion of the names of the minority people from electoral rolls on the plea of foreigners but the Mizoram election office could produce a fair and authentic roll on the basis of the general enumeration of the whole of Mizoram completed in April-May 1983 for the fourth General Assembly Elections. The furore caused by the issue of foreigners entering Mizoram (both from Bangladesh and Burma) drew the attention of the Central Government. Here is an extract from D.O. letter written by Brigadier T. Sailo, Chief Minister, Mizoram to Mrs. Indira Gandhi, Prime Minister of India:

Dear Respected Prime Minister,

"I am now writing this letter to you on the issue of the influx of Chakmas of Bangladesh into Mizoram. The Chakmas are Buddhist tribals from Hill Tracts of Bangladesh. Chakma Hill Tracts directly borders Mizoram. The Chakma population is of the order of 6-8 lakhs (population of Mizoram today is about 4 lakhs). During the British days i.e. before 1947 Chakmas used to apply for permission to settle in villages bordering the then East Bengal (now Bangladesh). The British Government used to sparingly grant permission to the Chakma applicants to settle in the Mizo villages with a clear stipulation that they were the subjects of the hereditary chieftains of the villages. The total number of Chakmas permitted to settle in the Mizo villages upto 1947 was found about 3,000 approximately. After 1947, due to various reasons, there was a certain amount of relaxation or slackness in watching the entry of Chakmas into Mizoram on the border. In other words, the Chakmas kept on infiltrating into Mizoram over the years and Mizoram Government were to put it bluntly, negligent in that no real check was made.

"In due course of time, the number of infiltrators became very big. Eventually, on account of certain 'political convenience of some politicians (vote catching game), the Chakmas claimed to form a small district along the Mizoram Bangladesh border which was conceded to. Thus a strip of land of the Territory at Mizoram along the border, has been made into a Chakma District, to accommodate foreign nationals. This was entirely a wrong action on the part of the then authorities."

Therefore, the foreigner issue continued to cast its ominous shadow over the Chakmas during People's Conference rule and this caused great mental distress to the Chakmas. In the 4th General Election in Mizoram, the People's Conference did not field its candidates from Chawngte and Demagiri constituencies where Chakmas are predominant.

The election campaign of Congress (I) got a shot in the arm with the dramatic visit of the Prime Minister Smt. Indira Gandhi to Chakma concentrated areas namely Chawngte and Demagiri. For the illiterate simple Chakma voters it was like a fairy tale that the Prime Minister of India took all the interest to come down to talk to the Chakma voters and that too draped in Chakma customary dress ! And thenceforth began the saga of success of Congress (I).

The Congress (I) came out successful with absolute majority and the results were as follows :

1.	Congress (I)	19
2.	People's Conference	8
3.	Independent	1
4.	Mizo Convention	1
	Total :	29

Out of total 30 seats, elections were held in 29 constituencies only since elections were countermanded in one constituency due to the killing of one P.C. candidate. In these elections Hari Kriste Chakma and Arun Bikash Chakma were elected as Congress candidates from Demagiri and Chawngte respectively. On being elected consecutively for 4 terms, Hari Kriste Chakma became the seniormost MLA among his contemporaries in Mizoram and by virtue of this seniority he was made protem speaker of the first assembly session after the 4th general elections which were held on 9th May, 1984.

The India Today magazine, in its issue dated June 15, 1984, carried a special report on Chakma crisis in Mizoram:

"In the jungle vastnesses of the south-eastern reaches of Mizo hills a new foreign national problem is taking shape. The Mizo leaders, who include the new Congress (I) Chief Minister Lalthanhawla and his people's predecessor Brigadier Thenphunga Sailo insist that region around Demagiri is being increasingly inhabited by the Buddhist Chakma Tribals infiltrating from neighbouring Chittagong Hill Tracts of Bangladesh. Said Lalthanhawla immidiately on being elected : Detecting and deporting foreign nationals will be one of the first task before my Government...

"In Mizoram politics Chakmas hold a lot of importance for the Congress (I) for which they have always voted, assuring two seats to the assembly. This makes things complicated for Lalthanhawla. If he continues the campaign against the Chakmas his party will lose their support. And if he is soft on them, the opposition will exploit the situation to rouse Mizo ethnic passions. For the Chakmas, thus, it would still be a no win situation".

The most vital Congress (I) pledge in the 4th General Assembly election was the restoration of peace in Mizoram which deeply impressed the minds of the Mizo people, as their earnest desire was to end the 20 year old insurgency in the state. So the foremost task of the ruling Congress (I) Government of the U.T. was to make the Central Govt. agree to take up the threads of peace talk with M.N.F. from where these were left at breakdown of negotiations in January 1982 while Brig. Sailo's People's Conference was ruling the Union Territory. Now, since the Congress (I) party was voted into power in the State, it was likely that the agreement could be reached with the M.N.F because the Congress (I) was also the ruling party at the centre delay accordingly a communication from the Central Govt. conveying its willingness to resume talk was despatched to Laldenga, President M.N.F. who was then living in Britain. Consequent upon this the President of M.N.F. made declaration of a unilateral cease fire with effect from October 2, 1984 by Mizo rebels for paving the way for resumption of peace talk with the Central Govt. to end the insurgency movement. Ultimately, Laldenga, President of M.N.F. assisted by the National executive committee members of M.N.F. sat with the representatives of the Central Govt. in New Delhi to work out a settlement of the Mizoram problem.

The discussions for settlement protracted for many months and ultimately the people of Mizoram became tired of the continued uncertainty. At one stage it was apprehended that the failure of the peace talk was likely to cause deep distress and undermine not only the M.N.F. leader's towering stature but also the position of Lal Thanhwala, Congress (I) Chief Minister of the State. But this misapprehension was belied by the outcome of the peace tak, since both the groups showed firm faith in each other which ultimately led to the signing an accord on 30th June, 1986 (the political part of it was signed on 25th June) between Laldenga and the Union Govt. (For the text of the accord and the agreement for formation of a coalition government which preceded it see Appendices I & II to this Chapter). Acting on the spur of the moment the Door Darshan gave a flash news item just after the daily newscast and immediately jubilant crowds were out on the street in Aizawl singing with joy. As a sequel to the signing of the memorandum of settlement, a nine member coalition Ministry of Congtess (I) and M.N.F headed by the Chief Minister Laldenga with Lal Thanhawla as Dy. Chief Minister was sworn in on August 21,1986. In keeping with the spirit of settlement, the Parliament on 7th August, 1986, passed the Constitution (53rd) Amendment bill and the state of Mizoram bill upgrading the status of Mizoram into a fullfledged statehood having a State Assembly with 40 members. To take over the charge of the new State Government, the General Assembly elections were held on 16th Febuary, 1987, in a peaceful atmosphere. The elections were fought mainly between Congress (I) and M.N.F. and the election results came true to the fullest expectations of the M.N.F. leader Laldenga who claimed to secure absolute majority. For Congress (I) it was a throw in the towel. The respective position of the different political parties in the State Legislative Assembly was as follows :

1.	M.N.F.	24
2.	Congress(I)	13
3.	People's Conference	3
	Total :	40

Laldenga was returned from two constituencies thus necessitating fresh election in one constituency which was also bagged by M.N.F. in the ensuing by-election. Therefore, Sri Laldenga, President of M.N.F. was seated as the first Chief Minister of the State of Mizoram inaugurated by the Prime Minister Rajiv Gandhi at Aizawl on 20th February, 1987 to become the 23rd State of the Indian Union.

As already explained the Chakmas hold a lot of importance for the Congress (I) in State Assembly elections. The election results once again brought this fact into light. Out of 13 Congress (I) members elected 6 of them could maintain their winning lead because of the Chakma voters. Nirupam Chakma, a Congress (I) candidate, was elected unopposed from Chawngte constituency. Another Cogress (I) candidate Hari Kristo Chakma was elected on Congress (I) ticket from Demagiri constituency. Chakma voters solidly backed the Congress (I) candidates in another 4 constituencies which helped them in their victory. Therefore, for Congress (I), the last pillar of support in Mizoram stands in the Chakma inhabited area and any neglect of this tribal community would be at the cost the six secured seats in the State Assembly.

This area is no less important for other political parties also to bring the wind out of the sail of Congress (I). Whatever may be the motive of all the different political parties, all of them make no bones of the fact that the fate of the Indian Chakmas of Mizoram must be tied up with the fate of the Mizos to shape a better future for all.

Chapter 9 : Appendices

APPENDIX-I

(Text of the Memorandum of Settlement signed in New Delhi on 30th June, 1986 between the MNF leader Laldanga and the Govt. of India)

MEMORANDUM OF SETTLEMENT

Preamble

1. Government of India have all along been making earnest efforts to bring about an end to the disturbed conditions in Mizoram and to restore peace and harmony.

2. Towards this end, initiaitive was taken by the late Prime Minister, Smt. Indira Gandhi. On the acceptance by Shri Laldenga on behalf of the Mizo National Front (MNF) of the two conditions, namely, cessation of violence by MNF and holding of talks within the framework of the Constitution of India, a series of discussions were held with Shri Laldenga. Settlement on various issues reached during the course of the talks is incorporated in the following paragraphs.

Restoration of Normalcy

3.1. With a view to restoring peace and normalcy in Mizoram the MNF party, on their part, undertakes within the agreed time-frame, to take all necessary steps to end all underground activities, to bring out all underground personnel of the MNF with their arms, ammunition and equipment to ensure their return to civil life, to abjure violence and generally to help in the process of restoration of normalcy. The modalities of bringing out all underground personnel and the deposit of arms, ammunition and equipment will be as worked out. The implementation of the foregoing will be under the supervision of the Central Government.

3.2. The MNF Party will take immediate steps to amend its Articles of Association so as to make them conform to the provision of law.

3.3. The Central Government will take steps for the resettlement and rehabilitation of underground MNF personnel coming overground after considering the schemes proposed in this regard by the Government of Mizoram.

3.4. The MNF undertakes not to extend any support to Tripura/Tribal National Volunteers (TNV), People's Liberation Army of Manipur (PLA) and any other such groups, by way of training, supply of arms or providing protection or in any other manner.

Legal, Administrative and other Steps

4.1. With a view to satisfying the desires and aspirations of all sections of the people of Mizoram, the Government will initiate measures to confer Statehood on the Union Territory of Mizoram, subject to the other stipulations contained in this Memorandum of Settlement.

4.2. To give effect to the above, the necessary legislative and administrative measures will be undertaken, including those for the enactment of Bills for the amendment of the Constitution and other laws for the conferment of Statehood as aforesaid, to come into effect on a date to be notified by the Central Government.

4.3. The amendments aforesaid shall provide, among other things, for the following:—

(I) The territory of Mizoram shall consist of the territory specified in Section 6 of the North Eastern Areas (Reorganisation) Act, 1971.

(II) Notwithstanding anything contained in the Constitution, no Act of Parliament in respect of—

(a) religious or social practices of the Mizos,

(b) Mizo customary law or procedure,

(c) administration of Civil and Criminal justice involving decisions according to Mizo customary law,

(d) ownership and transfer of land,

shall apply to the State of Mizoram unless the Legislative Assembly of Mizoram by a resolution so decides:

Provided that nothing in this clause shall apply to any Central Act in force in Mizoram immediately before the appointed day.

(III) Article 170, Clause (1) shall, in relation to the Legislative Assembly of Mizoram, have effect as if for the word 'sixty', the word 'forty' has been substituted.

5. Soon after the Bill for conferment of Statehood becomes law, and when the President is satisfied that normalcy has returned and that conditions conducive to the holding of free and fair elections exist, the process of holding elections to the Legislative Assembly will be initiated.

6. (a) The Centre will transfer resources to the new Government keeping in view the change in status from a Union Territory to a State and this will include resources to cover the revenue gap for the year.

(b) Central assistance for Plan will be fixed taking note of any residuary gap in resources so as to sustain the approved Plan outlay and the pattern of assistance will be as in the case of special category States.

7. Border trade in locally produced or grown agricultural commodities could be allowed under a scheme to be formulated by the Central Government, subject to international arrangements with neighbouring countries.

8. The Inner Line Regulations, as now in force in Mizoram, will not be amended or repealed without consulting the State Government.

Other Matters

9. The rights and privileges of the minorities in Mizoram as envisaged in the Constitution, shall continue to be preserved and protected and their social and economic advancement shall be ensured.

10. Steps will be taken by the Government of Mizoram at the earliest to review and codify the existing customs, practices, laws or other usages relating to the matters specified in clases (a) to (d) of para 4.3(II) of the Memorandum, keeping in view that an individual Mizo may prefer to be governed by Acts of Parliament dealing with such matters and which are of general application.

11. The question of the unification of Mizo inhabited areas of other States to form one administrative unit was raised by the MNF delegation. It was pointed out to them, on behalf of the Government of India, that Article 3 of the Constitution of India prescribes the procedure in this regard but that the Government cannot make any commitment in this respect.

12. It was also pointed out on behalf of the Government that as soon as Mizoram becomes a State,

(i) the provisions of Part XVII of the Constiiution will apply and the State will be at liberty to adopt any one or more of the languages in use in the State as the language to be used for all or any of the official purposes of the State;

(ii) it is open to the State to move for the establishment of a separate University in the State in accordance with the prescribed procedure;

(iii) in the light of the Prime Minister's statement at the Joint Conference of the Chief Justices, Cheif Ministers and Law Ministers held at New Delhi on 31st August, 1985, Mizoram will be entitled to have a High Court of its own, if it so wishes.

13. (a) It was noted that there is already a scheme in force for payment of ex-gratia amount to heirs/dependants of persons who were killed during disturbances in 1966 and thereafter in

the Union Territory of Mizoram. Arrangements will be made to expeditiously disburse payment to those eligible persons who had already applied but who had not been made such payments so far.

(b) It was noted that consequent on verification done by a joint team of officers, the Government of India had already made arrangements for payment of compensation in respect of damage to crops; buildings destroyed/ damaged during the action in Mizoram; and rental charges of building and lands occupied by the Security Forces. There may, however, be some claims which were preferred and verified by the above team but have not yet been setlted. These pending claims will be settled expeditiously. Arrangements will also be made for payment of pending claims of rental charges for lands/buildings occupied by the Security Forces.

Sd/-
LALDENGA
On behalf of
Mizo National Front

Sd/-
R.D. PRADHAN
Home Secretary
Government of India

Sd/-
LALKHAMA
Chief Secretary
Government of Mizoram

Date: 30th June, 1986.
Place: NEW DELHI.

SEQUENCE OF EVENTS

The Memorandum of Settlement contemplates the following sequence of events:—

1. Coming overground of MNF personnel and depositing of arms, ammunition and equipment by them in accordance with the time bound programme as already

agreed upon between the Ministry of Home Affairs and the MNF delegation.

2. The MNF Party should take immediate steps to amend its Articles of Association to make them conform to the provisions of law.
3. Government will initiate steps for rehabilitation of MNF personnel coming overground.
4. After completion of action under paragraphs (1) and (2) above, a Constitution Amendment Bill will be introduced in Parliament for the grant of Statehood and other consequential legislative measures to be taken up.
5. After the Bill becomes law, preparation for delimitation of constituencies and holding elections to the State Legislature will be taken on hand when the President is satisfied that normalcy has been restored.

Sd/-
LALDENGA
On behalf of
Mizo National Front

Sd/-
R.D. PRADHAN
Home Secretary
Government of India

Sd/-
LALKHAMA
Chief Secretary
Government of Mizoram.

Dated: 30th June, 1986.
Place: NEW DELHI.

APPENDIX-II

(Text of political Agreement on the formation of a coalition Government in Mizoram signed between Arjun Singh on behalf of Congress (I) and Laldenga on behalf of the M.N.F.)

Agreement Between the Indian National Congress (I) and the Mizo National Front Mizoram.

The Government of India under the leadership of Prime Minister Shri Rajiv Gandhi has brought about a situation wherein the long years of disturbed conditions in Mizoram are being brought to an end. The Memorandum of Settlement is being signed between the Government of India and Shri Laldenga, President of the Mizo National Front to give shape to this effort to usher peace and prosperity in Mizoram whithin the framework of the Indian Constitution. Shri Laldenga has pledged to bring the MNF into the mainstream of the Indian polity and irrevocably commit it to strive for a strong and united India.

In order to further strengthen this resolve and to enable a smooth and orderly transition, the Indian National Congress (I) and the MNF headed by Shri Laldenga agree to form a coalition Government. This decision shall be implemented in the following manner soon after the members of the MNF who are underground lay down their arms and join the national mainstream.

1. On a date agreed to between Shri Laldenga and the Government of India, Shri Lalthanhawla, the present Congress (I) Chief Minister will submit his resignation and Shri Laldenga will be elected the leader of the Government of Mizoram and be sworn in as the Chief Minister there.

2. Shri Lalthanhawla, the present Chief Minister, will be sworn in as the Dy. Chief Minister.

3. In addition to the Dy. Chief Minister four members of the Congress (I) Party shall be made Ministers in the new Government.

4. In addition to the Chief Minister, three members from the MNF Party will be made Ministers.

5. The names of the Ministers will be nominated by the respective political parties and the Chief Ministers will propose them to the Lt. Governor.

6. All issues concerning the formation and induction of this new Government will be decided mutually by the Chief Minister and the Dy. Chief Minister.

7. In order to smoothen the function of the Coalition Government, a Coordination Committee will be constituted consisting of the following :-

(a) Shri Laldenga - Chairman
(b) Shri Lalthanhawla - Vice Chairman
(c) Two members of the Congress Party.
(d) Two members of the MNF Party.

This committee will take into consideration all matters concerning the party and the Government which either of the political parties may deem necessary to bring for its consideration in order to help smooth functioning of the Government and to bring better coordination between the Congress (I) and the MNF.

8. This coalition Government will continue to function till such date when the President in satisfied that normalcy has returned and the holding of the elections has become feasible.

9. In the event of any difference arising between the two parties in the functioning of the Government or relationship between the parties they would seek the help of the Hon'ble Prime Minister to resolve the same.

Sd/-	Sd/-
LALDENGA	ARJUN SINGH
President	Vice-President
Mizo National Front	Indian National Congress

(MIZO)

Indian National Cong (I) Leh Mizo National Front Inkar Thuthlung

INDIA SAWRKAR CHUAN Prime Minister Rajiv Gandhi hruaina hnuaiah Mizoram kum rei tak lo buaina chu tihreh mek a ni a. India sawrkar leh Pu Laldenga Mizo National Front President chuan India ram constitution chhungah Mizoram a remna leh nihlawhna a awm theih na atan Memorandum of Settlement siam mek a ni a. Pu Laldenga chuan MNF te chu India hnam politic party tuipuia hruailuh leh tiamsut leh miah lo turin India chakma leh inpumkhatna atan a theihtawpa a beih tur thu a intiam a ni.

He thutihtluk tihhlawhtlinna atan leh hunkhaihlak fel tak leh thataka a kal theihna a tan Indian National Congress I leh MNF Pu Laldenga khihhruaite chuan sawrkar intawm siam an remti a. He thu hi MNF ten an silai an dah zawh a(surrender) India hnam uihna an rawn zawm veleh tihpuitlin a ni ang.

Hrilhfiahna : Hetilai thu atang hian kan hriat tur pawimawh awm te chu Pu Laldenga Chief Minister a nih theihna a tan leh Memorandum of Settlement sign fel a nih theih nan.

MNF te chuan an Silai te chu India sawrkar hnenah an pre (surrender) ang a, tin, MNF party pawh India political party tuipuiah chiah pil tur a ni. Engtinnge MNF party to chu India political tuipuiah chiahpil a nih theih ang ? MNF party constitution leh inkaihhruaina te chu Indian National Congress (I) duhdan ang thlapa siam a lo ni ta a. AICC Viee President Pu Arjun Singh a duhdan ang thlapa siam a lo nih tak khan MNF to chuan Indian Political party tuipuiah an zukfin ve ta a ni. Hetia Silai India sawrkar hnena an pek a, MNF party India political party tuipuia hnimpil a lo nih hian Pu Laldenga chu India sawrkar chuan Chief Minister nihna an pe thei ta a ni.

1. Pu Laldenga leh India sawkarten rem an tih tlanna niah chuan Pu Lalthanhawla Congress (I) Chief Minister nilai mek chuan banna a thehlut ang a, Pu Laldenga chu Mizoramah sawrkar hotu ah thlangin Chief Minister ah thutiam tir a lakluh a ni ang.

2. Pu Lalthanhawla Chief Minister nilai mek chu Dy. Chief Minister ah thutiam tira lakluh a ni ang.

3. Dy. Chief Minister bakah hian Congress (I) party chuan Minister pali (4) sawrkar tharah chuan a nei ang.

4. Chief Minister bakah hian MNF atangin Minister pathum (3) siam a ni ang.

5. Mahni party to theuh atangin Minister turte hi (nominate) ruat a ni ang a, chung Minister ruat te chu Chief Ministerin Lt. Governor hnenah a thlen (propose) ang.

6. He sawrkar thar siamna chungchanga thil awm reng reng te chu Chief Minister leh Dy. Chief Minister ten lungrual taka ngaihtuah tur a ni.

7. He sawrkar intawm hi tha taka a kal theihnan Co-ordination committee siam a ni ang a, chuta tel turte chu heng mite hi an ni ang.

(a) Pu Laldenga - Chairman

(b) Pu Lalthanhawla - Vice Chairman

(c) Congress party atangin Member pahnih

(d) MNF party atangin Member pahnih

He Co-ordination Committee ah hian Congress (I) in emaw MNF party emaw in Party thil emaw sawrkar thil emaw tul an tih ang ang chu sawrkarna tluang taka a kal theih nan an ngaihtuah ho thin ang.

8. Presidentin 'Mizoram chu Nunphung pangngaiin a awm leh ta' a tih a, Election neih nan boruak tha a awm ta a tih hun thlengin he sawrkar intawm hi a ding ang.

9. Party leh party inkara inlaichinna thilah emaw sawrkara thawh hona chung changah emaw harsatna thil awm reng reng chu Prime Minister zahawm tak hnenah a lo remsiam atan thlen zel a ni ang.

Hrilhfiahna : Co-ordination Committee hi kan en chuan Member inzat ve ve chiah an ni a, tin, thu harsa leh sawifel theihloh an neih chuan Prime Minister Pu Rajiv Gandhi an a lo tihfel sak thin dawn a ni, chuvangin he Sawrkar intawm hi Congress (I) thu thu a awm tur a nih a tichiang a ni. Tin, thil ropui tak lo lang leh chu MNF party te hian Congress (I) partyah rinna an nghahzia tilang chiang tu a ni.

Sd/- Laldenga, President Mizo National Front.	Sd/- Arjun Singh Vice President Indian National Congress.

Thubelh : Pu Arjun Singh a te Indian sawrkar aiawh zo pawh ni silo to hnena tlawm thu thlung zel zul khawpa tlawm chiang Mizo mipui te hi kan nih leh fiahna atan Mizoram Election lo awm tur hi Khawvelin an thlir thuap a ni.

CHAPTER 10

CHAKMAS IN INDIA : TRIPURA

The story of Chakmas coming down from Arakan along the river courses have already been narrated in Chapter-V and their movement did not stop there only as they moved from one river branch to another which ultimately led them into the state of Tripura.

The Chakma history records that the Chakmas crossed over into Tripura during the early Muslim period of Bengal. In the early 1600 AD, the kings of Tripura and Arakan were waging wars on each other for maintaining supremacy over Chittagong. At that time, the Chakma king Satrua was reigning in the south of Chittagong on the border of Arakan. The Chakma history has also recorded that the king became insane and subjected his people to various inhuman treatments and atrocities. Having found themselves under such a tyrranous regime the subjects rose against their king and ultimately killed him. (This story is known as the Pagal raja episode) The widow of the Pagal raja with her two daughters and some followers temporarily fled away to Tripura where one of her daughter was married into a noble Tripura family. This is how we get the earliest traces of the Chakma in Tripura and from that time onwards people in batches immigrated into Tripura in search of jhuming and cultivable land. A major exodus of the Chakmas into Tripura occurred during the reign cf Kaleendi Rani (Chakma Queen). In 1884, over 4000 Chakmas were reported to have crossed over into Tripura At the time of partition of India in 1947, a great influx of Chakmas took place into Tripura through the mountainous tracts and river routes. Among these various routes the hill tracts in the North of Tripura adjoining Mizoram bear distinctive marks of Chakma predominance even today. The following is the roadchart of these mountainous tracts :

Sl. No.	Place	Distance	Remarks
1.	Machmara (Pechartal)		This is the main cultural centre of the Chakmas in Tripura and is located on the National Highway on Assam-Tripura route.
2.	Machmara	4 kms from Pechartal	Chakma Village
3.	Kanchanpura	32 kms from Machmara	Mixed population
4.	Dhajdha	9kms from Kanchanpur	Mixed population
5.	Ananda Bazar	10 kms from Dhajdha	Mixed population
6.	Phuldungsei	18 kms. from Ananda Bazar	Mixed population
7.	Kawnpui	3 kms. from phuldungsei	It is on the hill top and 30 Chakma families live there.
8.	Tuipuibari	9 kms from Kawnpui	Situated on the river bank of Sajek in Mizoram, this village has concentration of Chakma population.

Sl No.	Place	Distance	Remarks
9.	Pansuri	25 kms. from Tuipuibari	Chakma village
10.	Silsuri	25 kms. from Pansuri	Chakma village
11.	Marpara	25 kms. from Silsuri	A village with a Chakma concentration.
12.	Begakhali	15 kms. from Marpara	Chakma village
13.	Samuksuri	12 kms. from Begakhali	Chakma village
14.	Howlongchera	12 kms. from Samuksuri	Chakma village
15.	Udachuri	12 kms. from Howlongchara	Chakma village
16.	Digilibagh	12 kms. from Udachuri	Chakma village
17.	Demagiri	18 kms. from Digilibagh	This is the principal cultural centre of the Chakmas in Mizoram.

At present an estimated nearly 40,000 Chakmas live in Tripura which constitute nearly 7% of the total population of Tripura. The Chakma concentrated areas are: (1) Satchand Development Block, (2) Chawmanu Development Block, (3) Dumburnagar Block and, (4) Kanchanpur Development Bolck. Most of the Chakmas live on wet rice cultivation or Jhum (shifting) cultivation. But since the jhumming land is becoming scarce day by day, many of them are moving out of Tripura in search of virgin land in neighbouring states. They are living in areas where Bengalees are numerically predominant and, therefore, most of them have adapted themselves to the Bengali way of living and habits. Many of the Bengali customs have become equally popular among the Chakmas in Tripura. Of course the assimilation of Indian culture in the life of the Chakmas is ages old. The Chakmas are originally Arakanese and they speak a language mixed with South-Eastern Bengali. This minority Tribe is bound to imbibe the cultural traits of the Bengalees in

Tripura. The Chakmas form a religious minority group in Tripura. They are ardent Buddhist in their faith and constitute only 10% of the total tribal population which also includes the Magh population.

There are a total of 19 tribal clans in Tripura. Their names and respective share in the total population of the state is as follows:

Tripura (Trippera 55.6%), Reand (14.5%), Jamatia (7.6%), Chakma (6.4%), Halam (4·3%) Magh (3%), Noatia (3.3%), Lu shai (.8%), Uchui (.2%), Kuki (1.7%), Garo (1.2%,) Munda (1.2%), Orang (.8%). Santal (.5%). Khasi, Bhil, Chaimal, Bhutia, Lepcha are all negligible.

The State Government has been very keen to ameliorate the lot of the poor Jhumia ethnic tribal group and with a view to attaining this objective it decided to establish the Autonomous District Council in terms of the Sixth Schedule of the Constitution of India.

Accordingly the Tripura Tribal Area Autonomous District Council Bill, 1979 was unanimously passed by the Tripura Legislative Assembly on March 23, 1979 and the Autonomous District Council in terms of the Sixth Schedule of the Constitution came into being in January 1982. Subsequently, the Parliament passed an Act to set up an Autonomous District Council in Tripura in terms of the Sixth Schedule of the Constitution. Its first general election was held in July 1985, and the same month the Governor of Tripura inaugurated the first session of the Autonomous District Council.

CHAPTER 11

CHAKMAS IN INDIA : ARUNACHAL PRADESH

In 1964, nearly 40,000 Chakmas crossed over into India and entered N.E.F.A. (now the State of Arunachal Pradesh) from their traditional home in the Chittagong Hill Tracts as a result of the inundation of their green patches in the valley by the impounded water of Kaptai Hydro Electric Project. An added reason was the religious persecution of the Chakmas by the Pakistani authorities and blending the ethnic Mongoloid Chakma community with the Bengali Muslims. Therefore, the history of the immigration of Chakmas into India is the tale of a disaster in their life which befell them due to swamping over of the Bengali Muslims into Chittagong Hill Tracts with the blessing of the Pakistan Government.

Chakma refugees crossed over into India with the motive of living with their ethnic brethren who had earlier settled in Tripura. They had a little knowledge of Arunachal Pradesh at that time. When they came to Tripura they learnt that the Government of Tripura were against accepting the Chakma refugees into Tripura. The Chakma leaders in Tripura left no stone unturned to gain the favour of the Government of Tripura for accommodating the Chakma refugees in Tripura, but all their efforts failed. Meanwhile, Shri Mahavir Tyagi, Relief and Rehabilitation Minister of India, accorded sanction for grant of cash doles to Chakma refugees who were willing to settle down in Bihar. But Mr.S.K.Chakma (one of the Chakma leaders in Tripura) vehemently opposed the acceptance of cash doles from Bihar Government as this state would not suit the Chakmas. At that momentous juncture Government of India was contemplating a scheme to accommodate a large number of Garo Sangma refugees in the no man's land of NEFA, now Arunachal Pradesh. Having become aware of this scheme the Chakma leaders called upon all Chakma refugees to settle down in NEFA.

The Chakma refugees then put up their camp at Manughat in Tripura. They moved in batches on foot up to Pechartal. On their way the police force tried to stop the movement of those refugees who had already received cash doles from Bihar Government, but their attempt failed in the face of the stiff opposition from the refugees (However, about 200 families had already been sent to Bihar by that time). From Pechartal, the refugees were moved to Dharmanagar by some hired lorries and from there they travelled by train and reached Ledo, the threshold of NEFA. The Government of India arranged to shift refugees from Ledo (Assam) to Miao Area (NEFA) and made them settled down at Diyun.

The Chakmas who came via Tripura were the first batch to settle in Arunachal. Their total number was 500 families only. Eventually, the majority of the refugees immigrated into India via Demagiri (Mizoram) only after the first batch had settled in Arunachal Pradesh. After Demagiri refugee transit camps were constructed with satisfactory relief work and from there they were taken to Manachara Transit Camp (Cachar, Assam). The flow of refugee continued all through 1965. After a year long halt at Mahachara (Assam), they were brought to Ledo Transit Camp in 1966 and re-settled in NEFA in due course of time. Many of them were resettled in the Deban area, a predominantly hilly, unirrigated and sandy area unfavourable for human habitation. Later, the Chakmas who had been sent to Bihar earlier were brought back to

NEFA in 1968. the government officials were appointed at Miao headed by a Base Superintendent (now called Circle Officer) to look after the refugees.

The total number of families rehabilitated in Tirap District was 1,976 with a population of 16,000. Nearly 300 families were settled in Balijan and Kokila area of Subansuri District and Chowkham area of Lohit District with an equal share. The population was estimated at 4,500 (approximately).

Thus, the Chakma refugees who were absorbed in Arunachal Pradesh were accommodated into three Districts, namely, Tirap, Lohit and Subansuri. They have settled there and started a new life and built a new society as ordained by fate. They found peace here as compared to the nightmarish existence in their erstwhile home in the hill tracts of Chittagong. Thus, they began a new life from a scratch in Arunachal Pradesh with dreams in their eyes. The refugees who settled in Debang area and lower part of Noa-Dehing Valley endured great hardships due to infertile granite soil which yielded one crop only. On top of this, vast erosion took place every year as a result of the course of Dehing river which ultimately led to the disintegration of the settlement. Consequently, many refugees were uprooted from their settlement area within a short span of time. Thus innumerable number of families turned landless and the Government of Arunachal Pradesh has not taken as yet any positive step for re-settlement of these refugees. They are in a sorry plight and have to struggle much for making both ends meet.

The Chakmas were absorbed in Arunachal Pradesh in the early sixties, but they do not enjoy the same rights as enjoyed by the local tribes. The fate of these Chakmas is still hanging in balance as they have failed to win the right of citizenship even after 20 years of their immigration into India.

There is not a single Middle School or High School in Chakma inhabited areas except a few Primary Schools which are also not adequate for their requirements. In 1982, All Arunachal Pradesh Students Union launched a campaign demanding not to give admission to the Chakma students into schools and colleges. To press their demand they had called "All Arunachal Bandh" from 17th to 20th July, 1982. This came as a great setback to the Chakma students. In the wake of this, the Chakma students had to go outside Arunachal Pradesh to pursue their studies. However, a small section of them stayed back in Arunachal Pradesh, but they were deprived of facilities like book grant, hostel accommodation, stipend etc. which are freely enjoyed by the local tribal students of Arunachal Pradesh. There are seven graduates but none of them could get a berth in the state government service. They are to seek a profession outside their own state. A doubt has arisen in their mind whether the local State Government was pursuing a policy of denial to the Chakmas.

CHAPTER 12

ORIGINS OF CHAKMA LANGUAGE AND LITERATURE

Pali language was exclusively used by the Southern (Hinayana) School of Buddhism in the pre-Christian era. It was the lingua-franca of the Buddhistic people. At that time Canjevaram on the eastern coast of India was a renowned centre of Buddhism. It is quite conceivable that there was an impact of Dravidian structural development on the Buddhistic language (script) which crossed over to Burma in ancient time. This inherent fact has been explained in the census report of 1891 by H.L. Eales, ICS, in Imperial series Vol. IX Burma report Vol. I, p. 62. There is a positive proof to show that Buddhism in Burma belong to Southern or Ceylon School and was first brought over by missionaries to Talaings (some believe that Talaings are from Telengana, India) of Thaton in 241 B.C., and that thence the missionaries worked their way northwards into Burma and eastwards into Siam (now Thailand) and the Shan States. Not only have we the Talaings legends, but also the acknowledged fact on the authority of Rhys Davids, that in the 5th century Buddha Ghosa (a Buddhist scholar from Buddha Gaya) brought over the Buddhist scripts to Thaton. Buddha Ghose sailed to Ceylon about the year 400 A.D. There he transcribed the scriptures and then brought them back with him to Thaton. At that time Kyaung Dayit was reigning at Pagan (north Burma), and most probably scripts or their copies were brought to him. At any rate it is an acknowledged fact that nearly 600 years after his death, Anawratha, king of Pagan, made war on Thaton for the possession of these scripts and conquering the town took away sacred books with him (32 elephant loads of Buddhist scriptures and 1000 monks).

This is how the Hinayana Buddhism from India/Ceylon reached Thaton (southern Burma) and thence to Pagan in the hills of northern Burma and later to Arakan, which is linked with the previous birth of Buddha himself. Before the advent of Hinayana Buddhism in the Hills (north Burma, Pagan , a corrupt form of Mahayana Buddhism had already been practised in the hills.

The Mahayana Buddhism developed in India as well as in China, Tibet and in Central Asia assuming various forms as influenced by local traditions, customs and practices. The custodians of the Mahayana Buddhism in the hills in Burma were known as Ari or Rulee (in local Chakma 'Luree'). In this form of religion strong drinks sacrifice of animals worshipping of evil spirits were prevalent.

The Rulees lost their powers when the king of Pagan gave royal patronage to Hinayana religion in the early 11th century. The Rulees finding it difficult to earn their livelihood adopted the village life.

There was no original script in the Burmese/Arakanese languages. The scripts brought from India (Canjevaram) has predominated in Burma/Arakan land. The scripts which has been handed down to the Chakmas from their forefathers bear distinctive similarity with the Arakanese script. The cursive style of the 13th century scripts of ancient Tamil has a great similarity with the Chakma scripts. The facsimile of ancient Tamil engraved in copper plates is given on the following page:

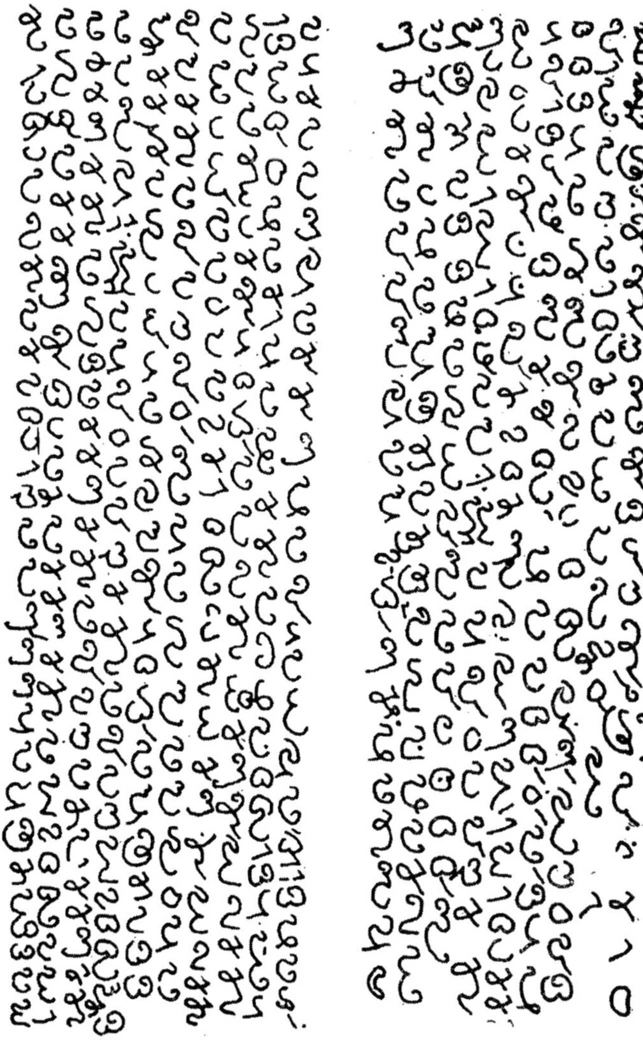

(THE 13th CENTURY TAMIL SCRIPT ENGRAVED IN A COPPER PLATE)

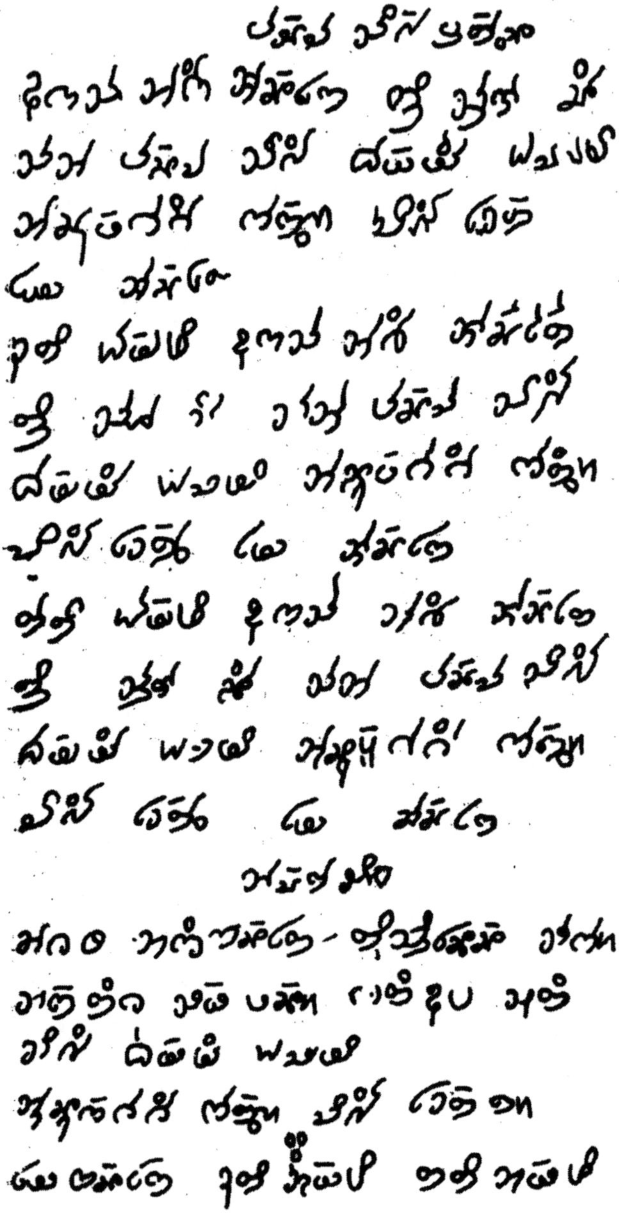

(CHAKMA SCRIPT)

CHAKMA NUMERALS

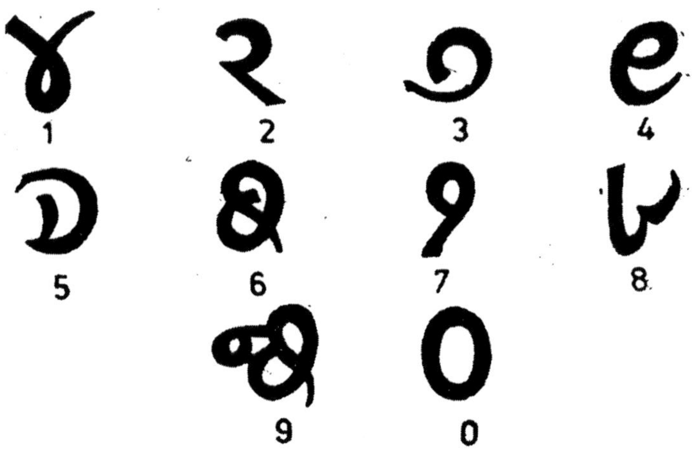

CHAKMA PRONUNCIATION SYMBOL

Sl. No.	Symbol in CHAKMA	Symbol in BENGALI	Use in CHAKMA	English Pronunciation	Example in CHAKMA	Bengali Pronunciaton
1	–	্ (ক্)	𑄇𑄴	K	𑄇𑄇𑄴	কাক্
2	।	ক	𑄇	Ka	𑄇𑄝	কবা
3	o	ি (ই)	𑄇𑄨	Ki	𑄇𑄨𑄝	কিবা
4	ϑ	ী (ঈ)	𑄇𑄩	Kii	𑄇𑄩𑄑	কীট
5	\	ু (উ)	𑄇𑄪	Ku	𑄇𑄪𑄇𑄨	কুকি
6	\\	ূ (ঊ)	𑄇𑄫	Khu	𑄇𑄫𑄣	কূল
7	(	ে (এ)	𑄇𑄬	Ke	𑄇𑄬𑄛	কেপ
8	>	—	𑄇𑄭	Kai	𑄇𑄭	কাই
9	ᴗ	্য (ক্য)	𑄇𑄳𑄡	Kya	𑄇𑄳𑄡	ক্যা
10	⌣	্র (ক্র)	𑄇𑄳𑄢	Kra	𑄇𑄳𑄢	ক্রা
11	o	—	𑄇𑄳𑄤	wa	𑄇𑄳𑄤	কুঁয়া
12	•	ং	𑄇𑄁	Kang	𑄇𑄁	কাং
13	:	ঃ	𑄇𑄂	Kaw	𑄇𑄂	কঃ

The earliest literature in Chakma script as available with the Chakmas is Agar Tara (a religious prayer in one book). These are practised by the Lurees in performing religious rites. These are written in the similar structural style as found in the epigraphic copper plates in Canjevaram. Therefore, we find that there is a great similarity between the Chakma script and the script that was found in the southern coast of India. Mr.G.E.Harvey has observed in his book 'History of Burma.' "What mnst have been a decisive factor was the rise in the 5th century after Christ, of a great Hinayana centre at Canjevaram in Madras under the commentator Dhammapala; ancient Talaing writings frequently mention Dhammapala and Canjevaram and the earliest Talaing inscription is in the Pallava alphabet used there in his time. The Burmese script was adopted from Talaing script and later it gave birth to the Arakanese script and the Chakma script is the offshoot of these scripts. This script is found in their religious book 'Agartara' and 'Gojenlams', the earliest literature of the Chakmas. The Chakma folklores or ballads like Genkhuli, Radhamon Dhan Pudi and Ubageet (love song) were composed in distorted Bengali, which indicates that they must have been composed much later after their crossing over to Bengal (14th century).

The present Chakma language has been defined in the Imperial Gazetteer of India Vol.I, p. 377 as follows:

"The Bengali of Chittagong is very corrupt and it is quite unitelligible to an untravelled native of Calcutta. Further, inland, in the Chittagog Hill Tracts, there is a still more debased dialect called Chakma, which is written in a alphabet akin to that of Burmese".

This is because of the fact that Chakmas have been living in the adjoining parts of Arakan and Bengal since very ancient time. Therefore, their language has an admixture of many Bengali words. Bengali language is a sister language of Sanskrit, which originated in the middle of tenth century only. Bengal (including Assam, the contiguous parts of Orissa and much of eastern, southern and northern

Bihar) became a distinct regional unit in the ninth century. The Bengali language has passed through two successive stages of development which may be called old Bengali and middle Bengali. It is now in its modern state. Therefore, we find many old and middle Bengali words in the Chakma language with little phonetic decay mixed with Burmese and Arakanese variety. In other words, the Chakma language is practically identical with eastern Bengal language and a large number of words are very similar in Oriya, Assamese and Bengali. Here is a list of words of every day use in each of these languages:

VOCABULARY

English	*Chakma*	*Bengali*	*Assamese*	*Oriya*
1. One	Ek (egwa)	Ek (egwa)	Eak	Eak
2. Two	Dui	Dui (dua)	Dui	Dui
3. Three	Tin	Tin (Tinwa	Tini	Tini
4. Four	Char	Char (Chargwh)	Chari	Char
5. Five	Pach	Pach (Pachwa)	Pass	Panch
6. Six	Chay	Chyhy (Chhawa)	Chai	Chha
7. Seven	Sat	Sat (Sahtwa)	Chat	Sat
8. Eight	Asto	Aat (Ashtwa)	Ath	Ath
9. Nine	Na	Nay (Nawa)	Na	Na
10. Ten	Dash	Dash (Daswa)	Dah	Dus
11. I	Mui	Ami (Mui)	Mai	Mu
12. You	Tui	Tumi, Tera	Jumi	Tume
13. We	Ami	Amara, Ayora	Ami	Ame
14. Your	Tar	Tomar, Torgo	Tor	Tumar
15. He	Tar	Sye, Tara	Shee	Se
16. They	Tara	Tahara, Onara	Sheehat	Semane
17. Mine	Mar	Amar, Ayar	Mere	Mere
18. Our	Amar	Amader, Amage	Amar	Amara
19. Him	Tar	Tahar, Targo	Tar	Tara
20. Their	Tarar	Tahader, Targo	Sheeha-ter	Seman-kar

English	*Chakma*	*Bengali*	*Assamese*	*Oriya*
21. Your	Tomar	Tomar, Tomago	Tomar	Tumara
22. Foot	Thanga Pada Pao		Vari, Theng	Pada
23. Nose	Nak	Nak	Nak	Nak
24. Eye	Chok	Chhook	Choku	Ankhi
25. Mouth	Mu	Muk	Mukh	Mukh
26. Tooth	Dat	Dat	Dat	Danta
27. Ear	Kan	Kan	Kan	Kana
28. Hair	Chul	Chul	Chuli	Bala
29. Head	Madha	Matha	Mur, Matha	Munda
30. Tongue	Jil	Jibba	Jiva	Jiva
31. Father	Bab	Baba.Bab	Bita, Deota Baba	Bapa
32. Mother	Ma	Ma	Ma	Ma
33. Brother	Bhei	Bhai	Bhai	Bhai
34. Sister	Bhon	Bhain	Bhani	Bhuni
35. Man, a human being	Marad	Purush/Marad	Manuh, Purus	Manish
36. Women	Mila	Mahila, Meya	Tirota Mohila	Maikina
37. Husband	Jamei	Pati, Swami	Swami, Pati	Pati
38. Wife	Me-eg	Stree	Stree, Ghaini	Stree

English	Chakma	Bengali	Assamese	Oriya
39. Child	Puya	Chotochele, Puya Chengra	Lora	Pipa
40. Son	Marad	Beta, Chele	Lora	
41. Daughter	Jhi	Meye, Jhi	Jee, Chowali	Jia
42. To come	Ajana	Asho, Astok	Aha	Ashiba
43. To go	Jana	Jao, Ja	Jowa	Jiba
44. To eat	Khana,Kha	Kho, Kha	Khowa	Khaiba
45. To drink	Gila, Phhona	Pan, Gila	Piya	Piba
46. Morning	Patya	Sakal, Phar	Patipua	Sakala
47. Evening	Belya	Bikal, Biyala	Godhuli	Shand-hya
48. Die	Mara	Mara	Mora	Mariba
49. Dear	Paran-no	Priya, Paran	Mormor	Priya
50. Bring	Ann	Ana, Ann	Ana	Aniba
51. Send	Pada	Pathao, Pada	Pathoa	Pathai-ba
52. Up	Ugure	Upure, Ugure	Uporot	Upana
53. Near	Kay	Kache, Kai	Ocharat	Nikata
54. Down	Tawle	Niche, Tawle	Tolot	Talo
55. Bad	Bajang	Kharap	Beya	Bharap
56. Good	Gam	Bhalo, Gam	Bhal	Bhala

Now from the above list we find the literary similarity of Chakma language with the Bengali, the Assamese and the Oriya (all of them taken as one unit). Dr. Sukumar Sen in his book 'History of Bengali Literature' has explained the literary tradition of Chittagong and Arakan as under :

"A close cultural contact between Bengal and Arakan, the neighbouring province of lower Burma speaking a Tibeto-Burman language was first made early in the fifteen century when Narameikhala, the King of Arakan, dispossessed by the king of Burma, came to Bengal and took refuge in the Court of Gaud (1404 A.D.). After a sojourn of many years he was helped by Jalaluddin, the Bengal Sultan to regain his throne in 1450 A.D. (mention has also been made of this event in Chapt. V of this book). We can reasonably assume that the king had acquired some liking for Bengali song and music, among other things, during his stay in Bengal and introduced them in his own country after he has returned home and to power. But there is no evidence to show how far this engrafting of Bengali culture in the Arakan Court was enduring, in spite of the fact that Arakan continued to be dominated politically by Bengal and its external affairs controlled by the Sultan's Governors in Chittagong. This position was however reversed for some years at least in the third quarter of the century when the Arakan power annexed Chittagong and kept it under its control until, in the first decade of the sixteenth century, it was recovered by *Nusrat Khan*, a general of Hussain Shah. During the years Chittagong was in occupation by the Arakanese it appears that some cultural contact between Bengal (and the rest of India) and Arakan was established. This cultural admixture is distinctly seen among the Chakmas."

The opinions of the linguists and scholars on Chakma language as recorded by G.A. Grierson in his well known book 'Linguistic Survey of India' are reproduced as follows :

CHĀKMĀ SUB-DIALECT

Over the greater part of the Chittagong Hill Tracts, South-Eastern Bengali is used as a kind of Lingua Franca, in addition to the many Tibeto-Burman languages current in that area. Among the wilder tribes, to the east even this means of inter-communication is absent, and a case is on record in which a woman of the Khamī Tribe once gave evidence in her own language, knowing no other. This was interpreted into Mrū which was again interpreted into Maghī, which was finally interpreted into South Eastern Bengali, from which version, the Magistrate translated the evidence into English.

In the central portion of the Chittagong Hill Tracts, in the Chākmā Chief's Circle, situated in the country round the Karnaphuli River, a broken dialect of Bengali, peculiar to the locality, and of a very curious character, is spoken It is called Chākmā, and is based on South-Eastern Bengali, but has undergone so much transformation that it is almost worthy of the dignity of being classed as a separate language. It is written in an alphabet which, allowing for its cursive form, is almost identical with the Khmer charactor which was formerly in use in Cambodia, Laos, Annam, Siam, and, at least, the southern parts of Burma. This Khmēr alphabet is, in its turn, the same as that which was current in the south of India in the sixth and seventh centuries. The Burmese character is derived from it, but is much more corrupted than the Chākmā. The resemblance between Chākmā and Khmer does not, however, extend to the typical peculiarity of the former that the inherent vowel of the consonants is *ā*, not *ā*, though even in this, there are noteworthy points of resmblance. The Khmer sign for *ja* has not the hook on the right hand side possessed by the Chākmā *jā*. This hook represents the *ā*. Similarly the hooks on the side of the Chākmā *ṭā*, *ṭhā*, and *rā*, are all relics of the old sign for *ā*. Chākmā is spoken by about 20,000 people.

The following account of the Chākmā alphabet is based on information provided by Dewan Kristo Chandra, a gentleman of Chākmā nationality, and forwarded to me by Mr. J. A

Cave-Browne, Assistant Commissioner, Chittagong Hill Tracts.

The Chākmā alphabet is as follows :—

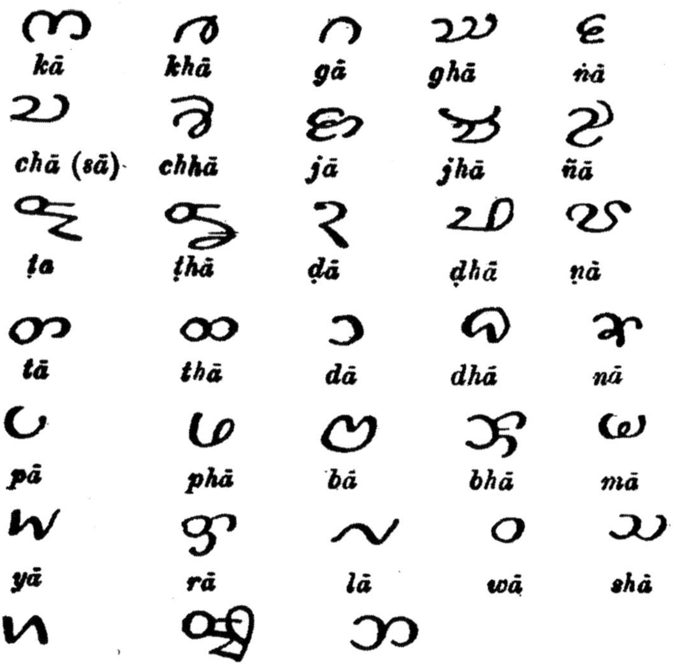

BENGALI.

The most important point to notice in this alphabet is that the vowel inherent in each consonant is, not *a* as in other Indian languages, but *ā*. Note also that 𑄃 the initial form (there is, of course, no non-initial form) of *ā* is treated as a consonant, much as the letter *alif* is treated as a consonant in Arabic.

For purposes of comparison, I here give the usual Burmese forms of the consonants :—

က *ka*,	ခ *kha*,	ဂ *ga*,	ဃ *gha*,	င *ṅ*,
စ *cha*,	ဆ *chha*,	ဇ *ja*,	ဈ *jha*,	ဉ *ña*,
ဋ *ṭa*,	ဌ *ṭha*,	ဍ *ḍa*,	ဎ *ḍha*,	ဏ *ṇa*,
တ *ta*,	ထ *tha*,	ဒ *da*,	ဓ *dha*,	န *na*,
ပ *pa*,	ဖ *pha*,	ဗ *ba*,	ဘ *bha*,	မ *ma*,
ယ *ya*,	ရ *ra*,	လ *la*,	ဝ *wa*,	
သ *sa*,	ဟ *ha*.			

As regards vowels, except 𑄃 *ā*, none of them have any proper initial forms. The following are their non-initial forms. In a parallel column I give the usual Burmese forms for the sake of comparison :—

Chākmā forms.	Burmese forms.	
𑄧 Over the consonant	None.	*a*
No sign	ာ or ါ	*ā*
𑄨 Over the consonant	ိ	*i*
𑄩 Ditto	ီ	*ī*
𑄪 Under the consonant	ု	*u*
𑄫 Ditto	ူ	*ū*
𑄬 Before the consonant	ေ	*ē*
𑄰 Over the consonant	ဲ	(*ai* pr. *oi*)
𑄮 On each side of the consonant	ေါ	*ō*
𑄯 Ditto	ေါ်	*au*

When a consonant has no vowel the sign ‾ is put over the consonant, equivalent to the Burmese ် and the Bengali ্. Thus, Chākmā 𑄇𑄴, Burmese က်, and Bengali ক্, all represent the letter *k*, without any vowel.

We thus get the following examples of the way in which non-initial vowels are attached to the letter 𑄇 *kā* :—

𑄇 *kā*, 𑄇𑄧 *ka*, 𑄇𑄨 *ki*, 𑄇𑄩 *kī*, 𑄇𑄪 *ku*, 𑄇𑄫 *kū*, 𑄇𑄬 *kē*, 𑄇𑄰 *kai*, 𑄇𑄮 *kō*,

CHĀKMĀ OF CHITTAGONG HILL TRACTS.

When these vowels commence a word, the non-initial forms are attached to the letter *ā* as a kind of scaffolding for the support of the sound, exactly as *alif* is used in Arabic. We thus obtain the following forms :—

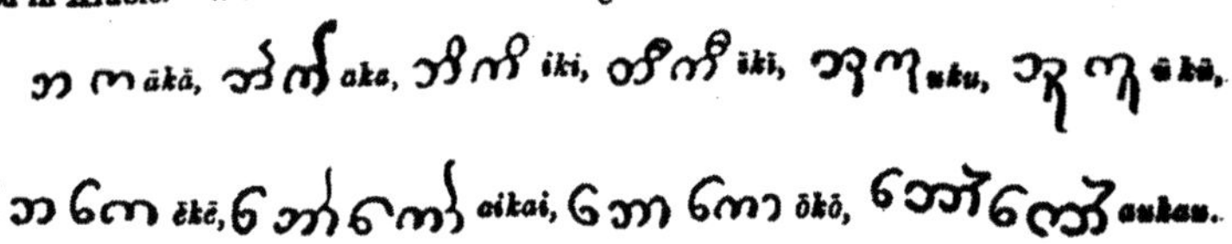

Note, however, that the initial form of *ai* is , not .

Sometimes vowels take special forms when initial. Thus we have for initial *ū* in *ūchchwā*, rejoicing, instead of . For initial *i*, we sometimes have as in *mūi*, I, instead of . Sometimes the form is used, attached to a preceding consonant, as in *bēida*, much. In the latter case may be omitted, as in for *jēinai*, having gone. Similarly stands for *ēinai*, not *āinai*.

The sign — is also used to denote the doubling of a letter as in *bhūyat-tün*, from in the field ; *ūchchwā*, rejoicing.

When the letter *yā* is compounded with a consonant, it takes the form as in *kyā*, anyone. In similar circumstances, *rā*, takes the form in *mantri*, a minister. Other compound consonants present no difficulties.

The letter *ch* is often pronounced as *s*, and when this is the case, it is so transliterated. Thus *bēs*, not *bēch*.

It is not necessary to give a detailed account of Chākmā Grammar, which closely resembles that of Chittagong. The following remarks will suffice :—

Cerebral letters are regularly converted to dentals. Numerous examples will be found in the specimens. We may quote, *dāki* for *ḍāki*, having called ; *thēṅ* for *ṭhēṅ*, a leg ; *aṅūdi* for *aṅguṭhi*, a ring ; *ghadaki*, a match-maker, for *ghaṭaki* ; and so on.

2 y 2

The Verb Substantive is conjugated as follows :—

	Present.	Past.	
	Sing. and plur.	Sing.	Plur.
1.	*āgi*, I am, we are.	*ĕlūṅ*. I was,	*ĕlaṅ*, we were
2.	*āgas*, or *ne*, thou art, you are.	*ĕlĕ*, thou wast,	*ĕlā*, you were
3.	*āge*, or *ne*, he is, they are.	*ĕl*, he was,	*ĕlāk*, they were

The conjugation of the Finite Verb closely resombles that of Chittagong. The principal exception is that the first person ends in *ūṅ* or *aṅ*. Other detail will be found in the list of standard words appended. The Conjunctive Participle ends in *inai*, as in *jĕinai*, having gone.

A brief Chākmā Vocabulary, under the name of Doing-nūk, is given by Phayre on p 712 of Vol. X, Pt. I, 1841, of the Journal of the Asiatic Society of Bengal.

CHAPTER 13

CHAKMAS : PHYSICAL AND CULTURAL CHARACTERISTICS, CUSTOMS AND BELIEFS

There can be no doubt about the fact that the traditional distinctive physical and cultural characteristics and religious practices of the Chakmas are not intact in their present generation as a result of their close interaction with the peoples of the plains, shifting habitations and change of political masters over the centuries. However, a majority of them are still living in the remote areas far from the hustle and bustle of the urban centres and some distinctive characteristics may still be discerned among them.

Physical Characteristics

Sir H.H. Rialey lin his Census of I ndia (1901) report, Vol. I, has definεd the specimen of Chakma as under :

Proportion of head (Cephalic Index)

Average	–	84.3
Maximum	–	96
Minimum	–	77
Range	—	19

Proportion of nose (Nasal Index)

Average	—	84.5
Maximum	–	105
Minimum	—	70
Range	—	35

Relative prominence of root of nose (Orbito-Nasal Index)

Average	—	106.4
Maximum	—	112
Minimum	—	102
Range	—	10

Stature

Average	—	159.5 cm
Maximum	–	169.6 cm
Minimum	—	149.0 cm
Range	—	20.6. cm

Indices (Head)	**Number of subjects**
Medium head	77 and under 77.5—3
(Meso cephalic)	77.5 and under 80+15
Broad head	80 and under 82.5–16
(Brochy cephalic)	82.5 and under 85–21
	85 and under 87.5–19
	87.5 and under 90—18
	90 and above –8

Nose	
Medium Nose	70 and under 75–2
Meso-rhine	75 and under 80+28
	80 and under 85–20
Broads Noses	85 and under 90–31
(Platy rhine)	90 and under 95–9
	95 and under 100–6
	100 and above—4

Root Nose

Platy-opic flat	101 and under 104 – 14
	104 and under 107 – 45
	107 and under 110 – 37
Mesophic (medium)	110 and under 113 – 4

Stature (Centimetres)

Short	under 155 (5″-1″)—19
	155 (5″-1″) and under 160 (5″-7″)—33
Below Mean	160 (5″-3″) and under 165 (5″-5″) – 33
Above Mean	165 (5″-5″) and under 170 (5″-7″) – 15

Chakmas are divided into 5 branches known as "Gutthis" according to the name of their progenitors and this hereditary line is again sub-divided into various gajas/clans. The names of *Gutthis* and gajas/clans are given below :

1. *Dhurjya Gutthi* – Dhurjya was the name of a chieftain who lived at Bak Khali in the district of Chittagong. The people of this clan are know as Baga gaja.
2. *Kurjya Gutthi* – The progentitor of this hereditary line was known as Kurjya. The people of this clan are known as Tanya gaja.
3. *Dhabana Gutthi* – The progenitor of this hereditary line was known as Dhanbana and the people of this clan are known as Mulima gaja.
4. *Pirabhanga Gutthi* — (means a low broken wooden platform for sitting). As the Chakma story goes, once a chieftain sat on a wooden platform which collapsed under his weight and since that time the people of this clan are known as Pirabhanga.
5. **Mendar Gutthi**-(means indignity)

   This gutthi has practically been forgotten by the present generation as the meaning itself aroused debased feelings.

Now the Gajas

1. Amu	16. Ichapocha	31. phedugsa
2. Bamu	17. Kala	32. phema
3. Babora	18. Kengrag	33. Pirabhanga
4. Barbwa	19. Khambe	34. Poa
5. Batalya	20. Khionjoy (henge)	35. Poma
6. Boga	21. Kura	36. Rangyacelumya
7. Borsage	22. Kurjya	37. Rangi
8. Bunga	23. Kutua	38. Sadonga
9. Bangza	24. Larma	39. Sege
10. Dhamei	25. Leba	40. Sekowa
11. Darjea	26. Loskra	41. Shoalyia
12. Dawin	27. Molima	45. Tuma
13. Dhabana	28. Molima-sega	43. Theya
14. Dhurjya	29. Phaksa	44. Toinya
15. Dhurjea	30. Phedangsiri	45. Uksarri
		46. Warggu

Physique, Appearance and Character: Chakmas are of short to medium stature with well developed muscles. They are hardy and can carry a weight up to 50-60 kgs for days together. They bear Mongolian features with yellowish complexion and little or no hair on the face and chest. They are happy people at their homes and give a cheerful look. They are honest and sincere people, but are sloth to change their old habits and usually do not express their feelings affirmatively. They are usually very spendthrift and do not practise the art of saving. Their requirements of life are very limited. They are very slow in making friendship with others and are introvert by nature. Their view of life is deeply rooted in their religious beliefs.

Ceremonies and Social Customs: They depend for their livelihood mainly on jhuming. Their main crops are usually rice, millet, teel, cotton, mustard seeds etc. They change their mode of living with the change of jhum cycle. The lean period of their economy comes just prior to their jhum harvest i.e. between july and September. They turn pauper in these hard days and become indebted to the moneyed men (mahajan, money lender). As a result major portion of their jhum yield goes out of their hand. The zestful period of their life during the year lasts for 1-2 months only i.e. immediately after the harvest. They are very hospitable and would entertain guests even by borrowing. Their ceremonies are usually of two types: religious ceremonies and ceremonies based on social customs. They believe in ghosts and spirits in their socials customs. They worship evil spirits and perform various pujas for being blessed with wealth, prosperity and happiness in their family. It is known as *Burpara* signifying various purposes. There are other pujas (ceremonies) known as *Ohys, Thanmana, Gangmana* which are mainly performed with a view to shielding the family or village against any unforeseeen evils. Witchcraft is also very common in the society which is usually made by a spell known as *Chalan*. Usually if a person becomes disagreeable then casting of spell to one another by *Chalan* or *Ang* would follow. Among the different forms of *Chalan* the following are the most common: (1) Bhut Chalan, (2) Puri Chalan and (3) Jadu Chalan. These Chalans and Angs are used for both good and bad purposes. For example, if a married man takes fancy of another woman, then the husband is to be treated with Eg-Garani Chalan, as a result of which the man would dislike his new lover and remain faithful to his wife alone.

Marriage: There are mainly two systems of marriages in the Chakma society: (1) Religious system of marriage and (2) Social and customary system of marriage. The religious system of marriage is usually followed among the advanced section of the society. This marriage is performed by the Buddhist monks (Bhikshu) as per the tenets of the religion.

The other form of marriage is very popular in the villages to this day. But due to the economic conditions not being sound much of their marriage display has been curtailed or given up. The usual marriage system followed in the well-to-do families is as follows

On a young man's attaining a marriageable age (say 20 to 22 years) his parents look about for a suitable match. On finding a suitable young girl of their choice, a male relative of the family of the groom will be sent to the house of the young girl. If the discussions are favourable then they will fix a day for a meeting of the parents of both the parties. The Bridegroom's parents should proceed to the would-be bride's house taking with them a bottle of wine. Eventually they will sleep in the would-be bride's house.

After a couple of days, the bridegroom's parents will pay a second visit to the intended bride's house, taking with them a bottle of wine and rice cakes.

Again, after some days, they would pay the third visit and this time with lots of wine, rice cakes and other eatables. On this occasion they will meticulously discuss the marriage topic. They will fix the date of marriage. On the day preceding the marriage, the bridegroom's party take with them presents, clothes and jewellery, and march to the strains of festive music to the bride's house. Then the bride is adorned with new clothes and jewellery and throughout the night there would be a festive mood in the bride's house. The next day, after the morning meal, the bridegroom's party escort the bride to bridegroom's house and in the evening the actual ceremony takes place. The bride and bridegroom are made to sit together, and two of their relations — a man and a woman — will, with the consent of all present, bind the couple together with a white cloth. the bride has then to place cooked rice and a prepared pan in the mouth of the bridegroom and he has to repeat the same act to her. As soon as the cloth is loosened they are declared newly married.

In the marriage ceremony a fowl is killed, its tongue taken out and according to certain marks therein, the following matters are predicted :

(1) Whether the matrimonial conjugal life would be happier or not, (2) how many children they will beget and (3) whether the first child would be a male or a female. The parents would also look anxiously for dreams which would indicate omen

and foretell the joys and sufferings in the married life of their children.

Polygamy: Polygamy i.e. the system of keeping more than one wife is also prevalent in the society. The marriage ceremony is known as *Chumulong*. The groom is to pay the price for the bride which usually includes paddy, domestic animals in addition to cash amount.

Divorce: The system of divorce is also found in the society and there is no barrier for widow remarriage.

Elopement of girls with their lovers is also practised and is considered as a more romantic method of marriage, but, if the father of the girl becomes stubborn and declines to offer his daughter in matrimony to her lover then no marriage can be performed (usually marriages are negotiated by parents and the women do not have right to choose their husbands). However, if in case the lover, for three consecutive times, can flee with the girl then the father of the girl would have to acknowledge the marriage and in that case usually the bride price is claimed at a higher rate. In other words, elopement thus not necessarily cancels the price of the bride, on the other hand, it only increases. Immediately after the marriage the newly married couple would receive blessing from their elders. This ceremony is known as *Seep Dan*. On the occasion of marriage, people, other than relations make presents to the newly married couple and this is known as *Seeuli Dan*.

Art and Music: Chakmas have not attained much proficiency in the field of art and music except for popular songs. Their old traditional musical instruments like *Singha*, *Dhuluk*, *Khengarang* have been replaced by modern Harmonium, Dhole and Tabla. Some of their old romantic songs known as *Ubageet* are still popular among them. The last remnants of their glorious historical past have been praised in their songs known as *Gengkhuli Geet*, *Radhamon Dhanpati Pala*, *Raja Sadeng Giri Pala* and so on. Unless special occasion demands these are not usually sung by them and before singing these songs the singer is to perform some prayers/ pujas in keeping with their old belief and tradition. There in no visible mark of their traditional dance style. Dancing is not encouraged in the society except by small children. As a result of their closer contact with the people of the plains they have developed the basic rhythm of dance which has become very popular among them. They are much fond of *Doli/Drama*.

The games of popular nature among the Chakmas are: *Ghila Khara*, *Nadeng Khara*, *Potti Khara* etc. which are still played with love and enthusiasm by the younger people.

Death: The Chakmas cremate the dead bodies. If the death occurs during economically hard days then they usually bury the dead body for the time being till the harvest time. When they are financially better off then they disinter the dead body which was buried earlier, for cremation and then perform the last rites which is usually follwed by a communal feast. In case a person breathes his last in the absence of his nearest relation like son or brother then the system of keeping the dead body suspended over the tree till the return of the nearest relation is still in vogue in the society. The head of the dead person in the case of man is set in the east direction while placing inside the grave; in the case of women it is set in the reverse direction. During the prime season of the year when the close relatives get together, they take out the dead body from the grave and cremate it by the river bank where the river usually flows into a curve.

The following morning some close relatives from the family of the deceased go to the cremation ground in search of foot-prints, which will he left behind (according to their belief) by the deceased person and that very shape indicates his re-birth. They are staunch believers in re-birth.

At daybreak the nearest members of the family (son, brother) of the deceased person get together at the crematorium and collect seven selected bones from the cremation spot and put them in an earthen pot and then they immerse them all into the river water after performing some rituals by uttering some mantras from the (*Agartara* a customary religious book in Chakma which is conducted by Ruli Badya village priest). All the sons of the deceased person shall have to shave off their heads at that particular place and then return home. Usually they observe seven days as mourning period and on the seventh day perform last ritual known as *Satdinya* by offering all their best they could afford to the Vhikshus who conduct the ceremony. All the villagers participate in the last ritual which concludes in a communal feast.

If the dead was a rich person, then his dead body is taken out ceremoniously on a chariot for some distance, before cremation which involves lot of money and material. This festival is known as *Rath Tana.*

AN ENGLISH VERSION OF CHAKMA SOCIAL AND CUSTOMARY LAWS

1. *Malik n'iya jharat kee jinishat daah jya laakaara deebar kah-daa.*

   A forest/jhuming area bearing a distinct mark of prior adoptation by any individual, shall not be possessed or destroyed (the said forest area) by other person.

2. *Jadeewa-ijjath-i tei kee-ki kam mana*

   Certain acts which are disdainful for the community and society as a whole are prohibited.

3. *Sadanga bei bone louya lui mana.*

   Marriages are prohibited with step-brothers and step-sisters, because the divine bond between them is much greater than any temporal relationship.

4. *Rana marde ki Ranee milai biya gari na parana.*

   After one's wife's death or one's husband's death one cannot re-marry till the ritual after 7 days in the name of the deceased (Satdinya) is over.

5. *Ek gosthi luya lui garana.*

   Marriage is strictly prohibited within the exogamous clan (gosthi). The gosthi transmits through male line. The woman changes her gosthi by marriage. Three consecutive hereditary membership through male line is known as three gosthi which is treated as one great family in the ritual known as gosthi bhat (gosthi feast). Marriage can take place within the same gosthi after the separation in 5th line of membership.

6. *Beena udshave na nachana, geet gana Oreng karana.*

   Restrictions on dancing, singing and rejoicing unceremoniously. The word 'Reng' cannot be adequately expressed in English. It generally means a voice (loud) of young man in the lonely valley made out of rejoicing, singing to allure his sweet-heart.

7. *Aw-chee-jeer Kha daa.*

   There are restrictions on expression or use of vulgur, ugly and indecent language and also on any obscene act in any public place. The word Aw-Chi-Jee connotes wide meaning. It also indicates impurity or unholy. In the event of any bad omen or evil befalling a family or village, the cleansing is followed through some rituals either religious or social. The whole of this practice is called Aw-Chee-Jee.

8. *Ghar-rh ba-hn, Para-ba-hn/kono Jah-ne bhangee deele.*

   Whenever an unholy spirit or a contagious disease attacks a family or village some ceremonies are performed in the whole of the affected area and such area is indicated by raising a flag, black or white in colour. The area remains closed for all sorts of traffic for some specified period. Any violation of this rule attracts punishment.

9. *Bya-jad-doober Kah-da.*

   The meaning of Bya-jad-doober cannot be adequately expressed in English. It may be explained in this way: The highest authority in the society is the king and even he is not authorised to enter with shoe on into the portion of a dwelling house.

10. *Bohu lonar bedhc.*

The system of marriage is called *Chumulong* (*Somo-olong*). It is performed by Oozah (Village Priest). In this ceremony fowls and pigs are sacrificed and the bride and groom sit together in reverence to these offerings.

11. *Gaburh mardeh-milai pagal ahle.*

On breaking of the sexual taboos by unmarried men and women the punishments are awarded by village elders which generally makes the offenders to offer pigs as fine.

12. *Kwhn dusath suwr deeya pare.*

On suspicion of indulgence in sex by those not yet married both man and woman are liable to be punished by imposing a fine of a pig. It prohibits free mixing in the society.

13. *Gausala Gung Puja.*

This ceremony is connected with the child-birth. Without this ceremony the mother and the child are treated as inauspicious. As soon as a child is born the father brings a basketful of dry earth and puts it close to the mother's bed and kindles a fire on it which is not allowed to be extinguished for few days. After this, earth is cast away; feast, amusements mark the occasion. Usually the mother goes to bathe in a nearby river on the next day of delivery, holding a rope of cloth in hand, one end of which is tied for fear of the evil.

14. **Under the provisions of the Chakma customary laws, the following punishments are usually awarded to the offenders :**

(a) *Jarimana* (Cash fine)

(b) *Muchlika* (Bond, Agreements)

(c) *Marpeet* (Physical Punishment)

(d) *Jendhera* : In this offender's hair on the head are cut into three parts and a fowl is hung on the neck and a bamboo broom is kept in his hand. Then he is escorted by two villagers to every house and on reaching at the door-step the offender shall pronounce his crime or misdeed for which he has been awarded the punishment. The offender shall also make sound with the help of the bamboo broom to attract the attention of the people. If the offender fails to comply with this then the escort is allowed to compel the offender to do the act under pressure and physical force. After having paraded through the whole of the village the offender will appear before the panchayat where his head shall be shaved off and then he will take a dip into water. After having done this the offender shall beg mercy of the panchayat. This system of punishment is called Jendhera.

(e) *Vandala*- In this the offender is to offer food with reverence to all the elders in the village.

(f) *Ham-o-Ladi Ujanee Lamonee garana* - In this the victim girl/woman after having taken a bath, with her wet dress on, shall stand putting her legs apart and then the offender shall pass through the lag 7 times - and every time shall utter her "Ma' (Mother).

Religion : Sir H. H. Rialey, ICS in Census of India (1901), Vol-I, p. 369, India—Part I, has noted that the Chittagong hill tracts is a professedly Buddhist district, and the inhabitants seem to have adhered to their Buddhism from very ancient times. Their adherence to Buddhism has already been discussed in Chapters II and III. Towards the end of the 10th century, at the time of Sen dynasty, Buddhism was discouraged in Bengal and ultimately during the 13th century Buddhism faced complete extinction at the hands of the Muslim invader and ruler Muhammad-i-Bakhtyar-Khilji. The inhabitants of Chittagong and Chittagong hill tracts in Bengal were the only people in India who kept the flame of Buddhism kindled in the holy land of India. However, this Buddhism had lost much of its life blood, as the dominant powers in

India were opposed to this religion. In the circumstances prevailing, there had been much amalgamation of practices or rituals in the Buddhism prefessed in Chittagong hill tracts. The original religion had been uprooted from the land of its birth India but spread to other countries. The Buddhism as practised by the Chakmas belong to the Southern school of Buddhism mixed with Tantrik Buddhism. There are two schools of thoughts in Buddhism; the Northern (Mahayana) and the Southern (Hinayana). Sanskrit is the vehicle of the former and Pali of the latter. The countries belonging to Mahayana or Northern school of Buddhism are Nepal, China and Japan, whereas Hinayana Southern Buddhism is practised in Sri Lanka, Burma, Thailand and India.

In the Northern or Mahayana Buddhism, it is believed that there exists a supreme being, the creator of the universe, called Adi Buddha, whereas in Southern Buddhism it is believed that a man even without any external aid from any superior being, is capable of attaining salvation, and Buddha is the highest type of humanity.

Hinayana is the oldest Buddhist doctrine and laid supreme stress on the attainment of Arhatship or Nirvana in the life, on the other hand, Mahayana is of later period, of 2nd century A. D. This school made a chief goal of the Buddhists, the attainment of Bodhisatship or the condition of future Buddha, with a view to saving all living creatures in ages to come.

In the northern hills of Burma, Buddhism has been mixed with Lamaism. This is called Tantrik Buddhism. Its professors are called 'Ari' or 'Ariya' in Burma and 'Rauli, or 'Ruri' in Chakma and although the Raulis wear a dyed dress (saffron-colour) like the Buddhist monks, they are not observers of vow of celibacy and can also pursue any kind of profession and trade.

Raulis perfrom rituals by reading and uttering some hymns from old clumsy records written in Chakma known as Agartara. This corrupt and clumsy practice clearly shows the great influence of Aris in Pugan (Burma) among the Chakmas. However, the Rauli system is no more prevalent in the present

Chakma society; there are hardly one or two Raulis in the hills of the Chakma community.

Vaishnavaism (one sect of Hinduism) was also introduced among the Chakmas at the advent of British era say from 1860 A.D. onwards. The disciples of Vaishnavas had made villagers separated from their kith and kin who were non-Vaishnavas. They took vow of abstinence from animal food and strong drink. They wore a necklace of Tulsi beads (*ocymum sanctum*) which is used to repeat the mantras. After the partition of India this sect of the Chakma community had been uprooted from its original source i. e. India and as a result their number have declined sharply in the community. At present there are hardly a few Vaishnava families in the society, but this religion had also left behind some visible marks in the Chakma society. In spite of all these, Buddhism is very deep rooted in Chakmas and 99% per cent of them profess Buddhism They might have little theology but have a great deal of religion. They call Buddhist monasteries as Kyaung and the monastery boy is known as Kyaungthaga (Burmese/Arakanese word). The historical precedents which made them follow many kinds of rituals have already been explained. Among the various forms of rituals and worships the following are the most prominent.

Burpara

This is performed every year to achieve wealth, happiness and prosperity.

Chumulong

This is performed every year by the married couple to renew their marriage commitments.

Gang/Ganga Mana

To shield the family against any unforeseen evils.

Many of their rituals are no more in vogue like *Thanmana* etc. as it requires participation of all the people in the village involving a lot of expenditure.

Witchcraft

Witchcraft is very common in the society which is usually practised by casting a spell known as '*Chalan*' or '*Ang*'. Normally, if some persons become disagreable then they start casting a spell to one another by Chalan or Ang. There are various forms of Chalans which are used for both good and evil purposes. A typical form of Chalan/Ang is produced below :

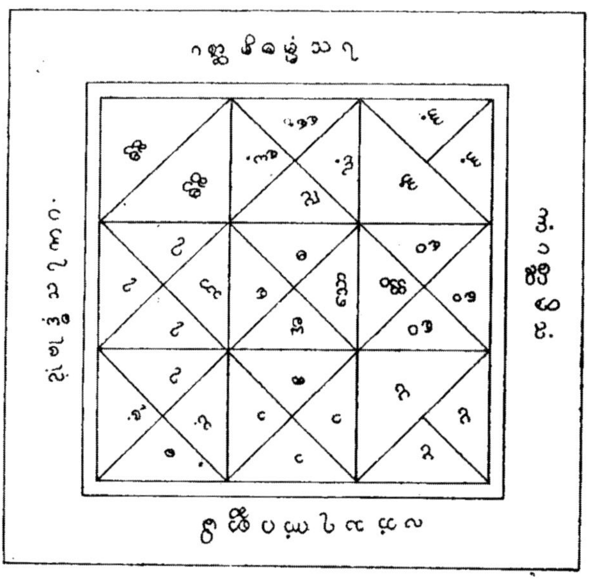

Sometimes the Chalans are administered in the form of tablets made out of poisonous jungle elements. Due to their such malicious deeds many of them die prematurely.

Chakmas bear distinct marks of old traditions of Buddhism. Every well-to-do family shall invariably construct a worshipping place (a small temple for Lord Buddha) in front of their houses raised from the ground on a machan. This religious place is always outside their dwelling-places. Their attitude to life is deeply steeped in their religious beliefs. They make generous offerings to Vhikshus, the Buddhist monks who perform all their religious ceremonies. In their daily prayers they take vow on the *'Triple Gem'* of Buddhism : *Buddha Dharam*: *Sangha* Sabbe Satta Sukhita Bhavanti, 'Let All Living Beings Be Happy'.

EPILOGUE

I would like to conclude this study with a few general observations. In the preceding chapters we have seen how the Himalayan mountains from Assam to Arakan Yoma played a very significant role in the domains of culture and civilization in the Indian sub-continent down the ages.

If we look at the map of india we will notice that Indian civilization is folded between the two river boundaries—the Indus and Tsangpo or the Brahmaputra. Indian races and tribes inhabiting in between these two river valleys are so deeply intermingled in blood that it will be impossible to discriminate them on the basis of skull characteristics or on caste or functional basis which came into usage in the later Brahamanical period. This civilization extended to and assimilated in its broad stream the ethnic races in between the valleys of rivers Brahmaputra and Irrawadi. This assimilation has been very deep rooted both from racial and religious points of view. The course of history would attest to this statement.

The earliest inhabitants of this tract were Thak, Shak or Chawk who are the progenitors of the Chakmas. The history of the Chakmas is a record of constant migration from north to south of the Assam Himalayan mountain range right down up to Arakan and Chittagong hill tracts. They have also moved westward along Tripura, Assam and again back to the north of this mountain range in Assam (now Arunachal Pradesh).

In the present age numerous tribes are living in the north-eastern zone of India. For ethnic and political reasons this region became home land for many of the tribes in India in the 20th century. Unfortunately, at that very crucial juncture in 1947, at the time of the partition of Indian sub-continent, the fate of the Chakmas was fallen differently. The unscientific demarcation of boundaries of a Hindu dominated India and Muslim majority Pakistan had forged the destiny of the Chakmas into ruination. Lately, many of them are trying to find their place in their original home land in India, but are being depicted as "foreigners" "outsiders" in many States in India today. It is an irony of fate that circumstances throughout history forced them to be on the move from one place to another. They migrated from one place to another and came back to the same place again.Not long ago, even when some of them were very positive and happy to have settled in Chittagong hill tracts, the country was partitioned as a result of which this hilly area was merged into Pakistan. The Pakistan authorities adopted a policy of a ruthless religious persecution towards the Chakmas. Their fate did not change for better with the liberation of Bangladesh either as the Bangladesh Government let loose unprecedented repression of the Chakmas to obliterate their separate ethnic identity.

In the entire passage of world history possibly no other race has had to face such an ordeal for their survival as the Chakmas. The Chakmas are now a scattered lot; each group trying to find a home of their own and who knows in distant future each group may lose its contact with other groups and finally in a slow but gradual process merge into the majority race finally passing into oblivion as a clan once known as '*Chakmas*'. We are to wait and see what the future unfolds for this race. Only time will tell.

Annexures

ANNEXURE – I

(Letter from the Commissioner of 16th Division and Sudder Board to the Collector of Chittagong regarding the Government attitude towards the Chieftains in the bordering hill areas.)

To

The Collector of Chittagong.

Sir,

I have the honour to acknowledge the receipt of your letter of the 24th instant together with copy of the order of the civil court called for by my letter of the 22nd instant No. 786.

(2) It appears that, on the death of the late Raja Dharmbux Khan in 1832 the civil court recognized the succession of Ranee Kalindee to his lands and possession, and on the 27th March 1833, the Collector recommended "that she should be left in charge of the Property" and that the estates should be recorded in "her name". The Commissioner doubted her capacity to manage the property, but it appears her incapacity was considered established because she refused to engage for some No-abad land the justness of the assessment of which she denied.

(3) In all parts of India these Jungles Rajahs are exempt from division under the Hindu law of succession, and it appears to me in every account desirable that the integrity of the

Raja should be preserved and opportunities embraced of strengthening the hands of these boarder Rajahs instead of weakening their authority. We can only rule in the hills by their means and they can be of use only when strong.

I have the honour to be

Sir

S/d Henry Ricketts.

Commissioner & Revenue Sudder Board.

Commissioner Office
Chittagong
The 26th August 1842.

(Extracted From Chakma Jatir Ilibritta, p. 196)

ANNEXURE—II

(Government Notification laying down the new rules and regulations for the administration of Chittagong Hill Tracts to come into effect from 1st May, 1900)

THE CHITTAGONG HILL-TRACTS REGULATION, 1900

CONTENTS

8. Chittagong Hill-tracts to be a sessions division under the Commissioner.
9. High Court.
10. Power to withdraw case.

CHAPTER IV

ARMS, AMMUNITION, DRUGS AND LIQUOR

11. Possession of fire arms and ammunition and manufacture of gun-powder
12. Daos, spears and bows and arrows.
13. Intoxicating drugs.
14. Foreign spirit and fermented liquor.
15. Locally made spirit and fermented liquor.

CHAPTER V

MISCELLANEOUS

16. Police.
17. Control and revision.
18. Power to make rules.
19. Bar to jurisdiction of Civil and Criminal Courts.
20. [*Repealed*]

Schedule.—Enactments declared in force in the Chittagong Hill-tracts.

REGULATION I OF 1900

THE CHITTAGONG HILL-TRACTS REGULATION, 1900[1]

[*17th January, 1900*]

A Regulation to declare the law applicable in, and provide for the administration of, the Chittagong Hill-tracts in [2][*Bangladesh*];

1 Local Extent.—This Regulation extends only to the Chittagong Hill-tracts—see s. 1 (2).

WHEREAS it is expedient to declare the law applicable in and provide for the administration of, the Chittagong Hill-tracts in [Bangladesh];

It is hereby enacted as follows :—

CHAPTER I

PRELIMINARY

1.—(*1*) This Regulation may be called the Chittagong Hill-tracts Regulation, 1900. **Short title, extent and commencement**

(*2*) It extends to the Chittagong Hill-tracts ; and

(*3*) It shall come into force on such date as the [Government] may, by notification in the [*Official Gazette*], *appoint*.

[2. In this Regulation— **Definitions.**

(*a*) the expression "Chittagong Hill-tracts" means the area known by that name as existing on the first day of January 1936 ; and

[(*b*) "Commissioner" and "Additional Commissioner" mean respectively the Commissioner and the Additional Commissioner of the Chittagong Divison.]

CHAPTER II

LAWS

3. Subject to the provisions of this Regulation, the administration of the Chittagong Hill-tracts **Chittagong Hill-tracts**

shall be carried on in accordance with the rules for the time being in force under section 18. how to be administes-red.

4. (*1*) The enactments specified in the schedule, to the extent and with the modifications therein set forth and so far as they are not inconsistent with this Regulation or the rules for the time being in force thereunder, are hereby declared to be in force in the Chittagong Hill-tracts. Enactments applicable in Chitta-gong Hi l tracts,

(*2*) No other enactment heretofore or hereafter passed shall be deemed to apply in the Chitta-gong Hill-tracts :

Provided that the [Government] may, by notifica-tion in the [*Official Gazette*],—

(*a*) declare ιhat any other enactment shall apply in the said tracts, either wholly or to the extent or or with the modifications which may be set forth in the notification ; or

(*b*) declare that any enactment which is specified in the schedule, or which has been declared to apply by a notification under clause (a) of this sub-section, shall cease to apply in the said tracts:

26 Geo. V. ch. 2. [Provided further that no such declaration shall be made after the commencement of Part III of the Government of India Act, 1935.]

CHAPTER III

APPOINTMENT AND POWERS OF CERTAIN OFFICERS

appoint-ment of 5. The [Government] may, by notification in the [*Official Gazette*],—

Deputy Commissioner and subordinate officers, (a) appoint any person to be the [Deputy Commissioner] of the Chittagong Hill-tracts ; and (b) appoint so many [Deputy Magistrates and Deputy Collectors] and other officers as it thinks fit to assist in the administration of the said tracts.

Investments of Deputy and Deputy Coll-ectors with powers of Deputy Commissioner, 6. The [Government] may, by notification in the [*Official Gazette*], invest any [Deputy Magistrate and Deputy Collector or Sub-Duputy Magistrate and Sub Deputy Collector] with all or any of the powers of the [Deputy Commissioner] under this Regulation or the rules for the time being in force thereunder and define the local limits of his jurisdiction.

Chittagong Hill-tract to be a district under the Deputy Commissioner. 7. The Chittagong Hill-tracts shall constitute a district for the purposes of criminal and civil jurisdiction and for revenue and general purpose, the [Deputy Commissioner] shall be the District Magistrate, and, subject to any orders passed by the [Government] under section 6, the general administration of the said Tracts, in criminal, civil, revenue and all other matters, shall be vested in the [1][Deputy Commissioner].

Chittagong Hill-tract to be a sessions division under the Commissioner, 8. [(1) The Chittagong Hill-tracts shall constitute a Sessions Division. and the Commissioner shall be the Sessions Judge and the Additional Commissioner, the Additional Sessions Judge].

(2) As Sessions Judge the Commissioner may take cognizance of any offence as a Court of original jurisdiction, without the accused being committed to him by a

Magistrate for trial, and, when so taking cognizance, shall follow the procedure prescribed by the Code of Criminal procedure, 1898, for the trial of warrant-cases by Magistrates.

Act V of 1898.

Act V of 1898.

High Court Division.

[9. The [High Court Division] [Bangladesh] shall exercise the powers of a [High Court Division] for all purposes of the Code of Criminal procedure, 1898.]

Power to withdraw eases.

10. The [Deputy Commissioner] may withdraw any criminal or civil case pending before any officer or Court in the Chittagong Hill-tracts, and may either try it himself or refer it for trial to some other officer or Court.

CHAPTER IV

ARMS, AMMUNITION, DRUGS AND LIQUOR

Possession of fire-arms and ammunition and manufacture of gunpowder.

11. (*1*) The [1][Deputy Commissioner] may fix the number of fire-arms and the quantity and description of ammunition which may be possessed by the inhabitants of any village, and may grant permission, either to such inhabitants collectively or to any of them individually, to possess such fire-arms and ammunition as he may think fit.

(*2*) All fire-arms for the possession of which permission is given under sub-section (1) shall be marked and entered in a register.

(*3*) Any permission granted under sub-section (1) to possess fire-arms and ammunition may be withdrawn by the [1][Deputy Commissioner]. and thereupon all fire-arms and ammunition referred to in such permission shall be delivered to the [Deputy Commissioner] or one of his subordinates.

(*4*) The [Deputy Commissoner] may grant permission to any person to manufacture, gunpowder and may withdraw such permission.

(*5*) Whoever, without the permission of the [Deputy Commissioner], possesses or exports from the Chittagong Hill-tracts any fire-arms or ammunition, or manufactures any gunpowder, shall be punishable with imprisonment for a term which may extend to three years, or with fine, or with both.

(*6*) The [Deputy Commissioner] may, with the previous sanction of the [Government], by order in writing, direct that sub-sections (1), (2), (4) and (5), or any of them, shall not apply in any village specified in the order.

Daos spears and bows and arrows

12. (*1*) The [Deputy Commissioner] may, with the previous sanction of the Commissioner, by order in writing, prohibit all or any of the inhabitants of any village from carrying *daos*, spears and bows and arrows, or any of those weapons, in any tract to be defined in the order, if he is of opinion that such prohibition is necessary, to the peace of such tract.

(*2*) Every, order made under sub-section (1) shall specify the length of time during which it shall remain in force.

(*3*) Whoever disobeys an order made under sub-section (1) shall be punishable with imprisonment for a term which may extend to six months, or with fine, or with both.

Intoxicating drugs

13.—(*1*) Whoever, except under and in accordance with a license granted by the [Deputy Commissioner], imports, exports, manufactures, possesses or sells opium, *ganja* or *charas*, or any preparation thereof or cultivates any plant from which opium. *ganja* or *charas* can be produced, shall be punishable with imprisonment for a term which may extend to [3][two years in the case of a person who has not been previously convicted of an offence under this section or to five years in the case of a person who has been so convicted, or with fine or with both, and shall also be punishable with whipping in lieu of, or in addition to any of the above punishments].

[(2) Notwithstanding anything contained in sub-section (1) any person may without a license granted by the Deputy Commissioner—

(a) Possess, for domestic use, one *tola of charas* or of any preparation thereof or three *tolas of ganja* or of any preparation thereof ; and

(b) if such person is registered under the provisions of the rules made under this Regulation as a habitual consumer of opium, possess such amount of opium or of any preparation thereof not exceeding five *tolas* in weight as he may be allowed to have in his possession at one time under the said rules.]

[4][(3) Nothing in sub-sections (1) and (2) shall apply to or in respect of "prepared opium" as defined in the Opium Smoking Act 1932.]

14.—(1) Whoever, except under and in accordance with a license granted by the [Deputy Commissioner], imports or sells foreign spirit or fermented liquor, shall be punishable with imprisonment for a term which may extend to three months or with fine, or with both. Foreign spirits and fermented liquor.

(2) Nothing in this section applies—

(a) to the import by any person, for his private use and consumption and not for sale, of any foreign spirit or fermented liquor on which duty has been paid ; or

(b) to the sale of any such spirit or liquor legally procured by any person for his private use and consumption and sold by him, or by auction on his behalf. or on behalf of his representatives in interest, upon his quiting station or after his decease.

Explanation.—For the purposes of this section, the expression "foreign spirit or fermented liquor" means any spirit or fermented liquor not manufactured or produced in the Chittagong Hill-tracts.

Locality made spirit and fermented liquor

15. Whoever, except under and in accordance with a license granted by the [1][Deputy Commissioner], exports or sells spirit or fermented liquor manufactured or produced in the Chittagong Hill-tracts shall be punishable with imprisonment for a term which may extend to three months, or with fine, or with both.

CHAPTER V

MISCELLANEOUS

Police.

16. The Chittagong Hill-tracts shall be deemed to be a general police-district with the meaning of the Police Act, of 1861] and [the ** Police Act, 1869] and the [Inspector-General of Police, [Bangladesh]] shall exercise therein all the powers and authority conferred on an Inspector-General of Police.

Act V of 1861.

Control and revision

17.—(*1*) All officer in the Chittagong Hill tracts shall be subordinate to the [Deputy Commissioner], who may revise any order made by any such officer, including [a Deputy Magistrate and Deputy Collector or a Sub-Deputy Magistrate and Sub-Deputy Collector] invested with any of the powers of the [Deputy Commissioner] under section 6.

(2) The Commissioner may revise any order made under this Regulation by the [Deputy Commissioner] or by any other in the Chittagong Hill-tracts.

(3) The [Government] may revise any order made under this Regulation.

Power to make rules

18—(1) The [Government] may make rules for carrying into effect the objects and purposes of this Regulation.

(2) In particular, and without prejudice to the generality of the foregoing power, such rules may—

(a) Provide for the administration of civil justice in the Chittagoug Hill-tracts ;

(b) prohibit, restrict or regulate the appearance of legal practitioners in cases arising in the said Tracts ;

(c) provide for the registration of documents in the said Tracts ;

(d) regulate or restrict the transfer of land in the said Tracts ;

(dd) Provide for the control of money-lenders and the regulation and control of money-lending in the said tracts] :

(e) provide for the sub-division of the said Tracts into circles, [and those circles] into *mauzas*.

(f) provide for the collection of the rent and the administration for the revenue generally in the said circles, andmauzas through the chiefs, and headmen;

(*g*) define the powers and jurisdiction of the chiefs, and headmen, and regulate the exercise by them of such powers and jurisdiction ,

(*h*) regulate the appointment and dismissal of headmen ;

(*i*) provide for the remuneration of chiefs headmen and village-officers generally by the assignment of lands for the purpose of otherwise as may be thought desirable ;

(*j*) prohibit, restrict or regulate the migration of cultivating *raiyats* from one circle to another ;

(*k*) regulate the requisition by Government of land required for public purposes ;

(*kk*) provide for compulsory vaccination in the said tracts ;]

(*l*) provide for the levy of taxes in the said Tracts ;

(*ll*) provide for the registration of persons who are habitual consumers of opium in the said Tracts ; and]

(*m*) regulate the procedure to be observed by officers acting under this Regulation or the rules for the time being in force thereunder.

(*3*) All rules made by the [Government] under this section shall be published in the [*official Gazette*] and on such publication, shall have effect as if enacted by this Regulation.

(*4*) The powers conferred by this section on the [Government] shall be powers of the [Government] as respects rules for the regulation of the following matters, namely—

(*a*) the possession of fire-arms and ammunition and the manufacture of gunpowder ;

(*b*) the cultivation, manufacture and sale for export of opium and ;

(*c*) the import or export across customs frontiers as defined by the [Government], of any intoxicating drug of foreign spirit or fermented liquor.]

Bar to jurisdiction Civil and Criminal Courts

19. Except as provided in this regulation or in of any other enactment for the time being in force, a decision passed, act done or order made under this Regulation or the rules thereunder, shall not be called in question in any Civil or Criminal Court.

20. [*Repeal of certain enactments.*] *Rep. by the Amending Act, 1903* (*I of 1903*).

The Chittagong Hill-tracts Regulation, 1900

THE SCHEDULE (*See section 4*)

Enactments Declared in Force in the Chittagong Hill-Tracts

Year 1	No. 2	Short title or subject 3	Extent of application 4	Modifications 5
		1—Acts of the Governor-General-in Council		
1843	V	The Slavery Act, 1843	So much as may from time to time, be in force in the district of Chittagong.	
1850	XVIII	The Judicial Officers' Protection Act, 1850.	Ditto.	
1850	XXXIV	The state Prisoners Act, 1850.	Ditto.	
1857	XI	The State Offences Act, 1857.	Ditto.	
1858	III	The State Prisoners Act, 1858.	Ditto.	
1860	XLV	The[1] Penal Code.	Ditto.	
1861	V	The Police Act, 1861.	Ditto.	
1864	VI	The Whipping Act, 1864.	Ditto.	
			Whipping in lieu of, or in addition to, other punishment.	For section 6 the following shall be *substituted*, namely:- "6. Notwithstanding anything in the foregoing section, a person convicted of any offence may be punished with whipping in lieu of, or in addition to, any other punishment to which he may be liable."

1. The word "Pakistan" in the tittle be read as omitted by P.O. No. 48 of 1972.

The Schedule—Contd.

Year 1	No. 2	Short title or subject 3	Extent of application. 4	Modifications 5
1872	I	The Evidence Act, 1872 3	So much as may from time to time, be in force in the district of Chittagong.	
1877	XV	The Limitation Act, 1877.	Ditto.	
1*	*	* * * *		
1879	VI	The Elephants Preservation Act, 1879.	Ditto.	
1897	X	The General Clauses Act, 1897.	[So far as it is not inconsistent with this Regulation, or the rules framed hereunder.]	
1898	V	The Code of Criminal Procedure, 1898.	So much as may, from time to time be in force in the district of Chittagong.	Nothing in the Code shall apply to cases tried by the chiefs, 3* or headmen in exercise of the powers conferred upon them by rules made under section 18 of this Regulation.

1. The entries relating to the Indian Forest Act, 1878 were *omitted* by Bengal Regulation V of 1942, s. 4.

2. The expression within square brackets was *substituted* in column 4 against entry No. 13 of the Schedule for the expression "So much as may, from time to time, be in force in the district of Chittagong" by the Chittagong Hill-tracts (Amendment) Regulation, 1960 (E.P. Reg. 111 of 1960), s. 2.

3. The word "*diwans*" was *repealed* by the Repealing and Amending Act, 1927 (X of 1927).

The Schedule. Contd.

Year 1	No. 2	Short title or subject 3	Extent of application 4	Modifications 5
1898	VI	The Post Office Act, 1898.	So much as may, from time to time, be in force in the district of Chittagong.	[1](*1*) The proviso to sub-section (1) of section 7 and the First Schedule shall be *omitted*. (2) *For* sub-section (2 of section 7. the following shall be *substituted*, namely :– "(*2*) unless and until such notification as aforesaid is issued the rates chargeable for the time being in the rest of British India shall be the rates chargeable in the Chittagong Hill-tract".
2.—Acts of the Lieutenant-Governor of Bengal in Council.				
1869	VII	Police	So much as may, from time to time, be in force in the district of Chittagong.	
1899	I	*The Bengal General Clauses Act, 1899*[2].	Ditto.	

1. This entry was *inserted* in column 5 of the Schedule to this Regulation against the entry relating to the "The Post Office Act,, 1898" and shall be deemed always to have been *inserted* by section 3 of the Bengal Regulation 11 of 1942.

2. Bengal Act 1 of 1899 is *repealed* in the Chittagong Hill-tracts by s. 2 of the Eastern Bengal and Assam General Clauses Act, 1909 (E.B. and A Act 1 of 1909).

The Schedule. Contd.

3.—Regulation of the Bengal Code

Year 1	No. 2	Short title or subject 3	Extent of application 4	Modifications 5
1818	III	The Bengal State prisoners Regulation, 1818	So much as may, from time to time, be in force in the district of Chittagong.	
		4.—Regulation Made under he government of India Aet, 1870 (33 VICT., c. 3.)		
1881	III	The Chittagong Hill-tracts Frontier Police Regulation 1881.	... ...	[1]* * *

1. The entry in column 5 was *omitted* by s. 6 of the Chittagnong Hill-tracts (Amendment) Regulation, 1920 (Reg. IV of 1920).

ANNEXURE – III

(An open letter dated 25.11,83 to Lt. General H.M. Ershad, Chief Martial Law Administrator of Bangladesh by the Shanti Bahini drawing his attention to the manifold problems faced by the people of the Chittagong Hill Tracts.)

An Open Letter

To Lt. General Ershad, Chief Martial-Law Administrator of Bangladesh On His October 3 Proclamation

Most Honourable Chief Martial-law Administrator.

Your Proclamation as Chief Martial-law Administrator of Bangladesh form the Rangamati Stadium in Chittagong Hill Tracts on October 3, 1983 was heard by the Shanti Bahini or the Jana Samhati Samity with extreme pleasure. From this High Power Proclamation it is evident that the problems and affairs of Chittagong Hill Tracts have posed a national crisis to your country.

You have proclaimed to the socalled "misguided tribal youths" a General Amnesty attended with Rs. 5000/-each and a yearlong weekly ration of 21 seers. You have also offered them Rs. 7000/- for each L.M.G., Rs. 5000/- for each S.M.C./S.M.G., Rs 3000/- for each Rifle, Rs 1000/- for each Pistol, Rs. 100/- for each Granade of Pound of explosive and Re 1/- for each Bullet, besides lofty Rehabilition, and proclaimed, "The easier we can assimilate the misguided youngmen, the sooner shall all the problems be resolved !" It was, as it were, you and your Government were determined to build a paradise for the Jumma Peoples of Chittagong Hill Tracts !

But Honourable Sir, you have nowhere declared your PROBLEMS themselves ! Instead, you have proclaimed, "Government have declared Chittagong Hill Tracts a Special Economic Zone !" and "Only for Chittagong Hill Tracts a Five year Plan has been undertaken !" etc.

Hon'ble General, the members of the Shanti-Bahini/Jana Samhati Samity have not been moving underground with begging bowls to feast in jungle hideouts for years together. The members of the Shanti Bahini did not take up Arms in order to make good trade with your Government at high premium.

Hon'ble Chief Martial-law Administrator, you have tried enormously to torture your predecessors by proclaiming—"For long, this area was neglected, and was deprived of developments; I want to resolve all those deprivations !" But do you and your Government propose to recompense the deprivation of the Jumma Peoples of Chittagong Hill Tracts from their Rights, Safeguards and very Existence—

by illegal infiltration of thousands of Mussalmans into this Non-Muslim area and forcefully giving them lands ?

by forcing in such enactments as would legalize Muslim occupation of lands in Chittagong Hill Tracts ?

by sending enormous Military Expeditions into our entire area ?

by imprisoning the Jumma Peoples into the socalled 'Collective' and 'Ideal' Villages for making room for Mussulmans ?

Then you rose a step further on humane rapture and declared, "We are part and parcel of a same race ! Our relation is a blood relation..........." where we could read your terrible writing on the wall that you will in no time, liquidate the ethnic identity, traditional, linguistic and cultural distinction of the Jumma Peoples.

You have been ecstatic in proclaiming. "The British made Hill Tracts Manual of 1900 A.D. today awaits modification, reformation and thorough development. Government shall present a revised Manual suited to the Hills People without delay". But you and your Government know that your previous Governments had been in successive plots cunningly to steal and infringe the rights and safeguards of the Jumma Peoples embodied in the Manual of 1900 A.D. with the set purpose of crushing the racial, religious, cultural and traditional identity and distinction destroying the very security and existence of the Ethnic Minority Nationalities of Chittagong Hill Tracts. Consequently, the Jumma Peoples were compelled to organize a Movement for ensuring their National Identity and the integrity of their Motherland. But circumstances so led them that at last, a full decade ago, they had to take to Arms in demand of SELFDETERMINATION.

The wide world knows that the Governments of Bangladesh had been waging a REGULAR WARFARE in secret against the Jana Samhati Samity, i.e. the JUMMA PEOPLES of Chittagong Hill Tracts where 50% of the Bangladesh Forces have been deployed. But you have bluffed the world saying that it was just an internal law & order situation of Bangladesh.

And, today, from an innocent platform, you are pleased to announce a socalled 'revised Manual' for the Jumma Peoples without any consultation with them, behind which you have the same sinister motive of your predecessors to abolish the protective laws of the Hill Tracts Manual of 1900, with a novel trickery.

BUT

Most Exalted Chief Martial-law Administrator.

On October 3, 1900, in Ranamati, with authoritative pride, you did proclaim—

"My Proclamation of this Amnesty—is not a sign of weakness ! If need be, I will continue to WAR for hundred thousand years ! I will preserve my country's INDEPENDENCE and SOVEREIGNTY !"

Good Sir, for the first time, you and your Government are pleased to CONFESS that the Bangladesh Forces are engaged in a REGULAR WARFARE aganist the SHANTI BAHINI of the Parbatya Chattagram Jana Samhati Samity with the I'DEPENDENCE SOVEREIGNTY of BANGLADESH at stake ! This CONFESSION of your honour has, doubtlessly added to the dignity of the Jumma Peoples,

But why this WAR ?

What do the Jumma Peoples want ? And why is the Jana Smhati Samity engaged in a WAR of SELFDETERMINATION,

That, Sir, in consonance with your predecessors, you and your Government had never minded to investigate and appreciate these FUNDAMENTAL QUESTIONS, and that you are decidedly unwilling to solve the Problems of the Jumma Peoples on PRINCIPLE & JUSTICE--has been very clearly proved by your October 3 proclamation, an embodiment of Surreptitious plans, Election Demagogy, Political Debauchery and Heinous Conspiracy— which may only create a temporary confusion, but, by which the Demand of the Juma Peoples for Salfdetermination can never by subsided.

The War of Selfdetermination shall run unabated.

Thanking you,
Central Executive,
Jana Samhati Samity,
Chittagong Hill Tracts.

Date : November 25, 198?.

ANNEXURE – IV

(Report published in a London based paper on the policy of racism in the Chittagong Hill Tracts)

8/16 CORONET STREET OFF OLD STREET VOL.366
LONDON N.I. 6HD

Racism in Chittagong

There, the 13 tribes of the Chittagong Hill Tracts are different from the majority Bangali Muslim population in many obvious ways. In appearance, they have more in common with the Burmese, in religion. they are mostly Buddhist, and Bengali is not their first language. They are people of the hills and not of the plains; they are not traders but farmers concerned with growing food for their families and not for sale at a profit; and land, which has a special spiritual significance for them, is mostly held in common.

The hillsmen of the Chittagong Hill Tracts are conscious of their difference from the Bengalis and cling with pride to their way of life. A way of life, it is worth emphasizing, which is in sympathy with nature and which is beneficial to the environment. The tribespeople make up less than one per cent of the total population of Bangladesh and it is the smalness of their number which contributes to their vulnerability. Prejudice thrives on the weakness of minorities and it goes on the rampage when it is condoned or at least not seen to be actively countered by a military Government.

In March 1980, at the tracts town of Kaokhali Bazar, a small detachment of the Bangladeshi army ordered leading tribes people to gather in the square and then shot them. The exact number of the dead is not known, but at least 5o people are buried in mass graves at the western corner of Poapara High School, just behind the army camp.

Although martial law was not imposed on Bangladesh until March 1932, the 5,000 square milles of the hill tracts have been under military rule undeclared, illegal but nevertheless real and effective, since their "special status" was abolished by Dhaka in 1972.

This status was codified and protected during the days of the British Raj and in fact the tribespeople had a large measure of independence during the Mughal Raj. Until 1964, the hill people had enjoyed wide powers of self-government, had collected their own taxes and run their own police force. Entry into the hills by non-tribespeople had been rigidly controlled and the hillmen had always made up nearly 100 per cent of the population there. Now they are just over half of the people living in the tracts and if Government policy of offering land and other inducements to settlers is not changed, they will soon be outnumbered by Bengalis. They will become, a minority not just in Bangladesh, but in their own homelands.

After independence in 1947 and, with increasing speed after 1964, the tribespeople lost control over their land, their lives and their future. Since the 1970s an undeclared but bloody war between them and an alliance of Bangladeshi soldiers and Bengali settlers has been taking place. Since 1976 the number of police stations (manned, of course, by Bengalis) has more than doubled; there are at least 100,000 members of the armed forces in the tracts; checkposts are commonplace and visible evidence of a form of occupation run by the G.O.C. Chittagong. Although settlers are actively encouraged, journalists and visitors are banned.

Bangladesh is a desperately poor and overcrowded country and the promise of "development", especially when made possible by loans from such bodies as the World Bank and

Asian Development Bank, must seem irresistible to the bureaucrats of Dhaka. But what is the price of development in human terms ?

In 1962 one of the sub-continent's most ambitious hydro-electric schemes was completed at Karnaphuli, deep hill tracts. It is the country's major source of electricity, but the electricity, bypasses the tribespeople. The artificial lake created behind the dam submerged 40 per cent of the best agricultural land traditionally farmed by the hillmen. The projects as a whole displaced 100,000 people, about a sixth of the tribal population. They were not consulted before work began and they were often removed at gunpoint. No one was adequately compensated and many are still waiting for even a token recompenses. Most of these families have become landless wanderers as no alternative land was provided for them by the Government.

Because the authorities of Bangladesh offer them no protection, the minorities of the Chittagong Hill Tracts are now fighting back and a militia, the Shanti Bahini, is their only ground defence

If the unrest in the hill tracts is really just the reaction of people to change which, according to the official stand taken by Dhaka, is for the greater economic good of Bangladesh as a whole, then what is the justification for such acts as the desecration of temples and the attacks on Buddhist priests? Is it progress, an unavoidable byproduct of development, to slaughter a cow on the saffron robe of a monk ? This happened in the Kattali Temple, 70 miles north-east of the hill tracts town of Rangamati.

Economic change is often accompanied by human casualties. But are the almost daily occurrences of rape and bloodshed and arbitrary arrest simply such casualties ? Or it is something else happening in the Chittagong Hill Tracts ?

ANNEXURE—V

(An extract from a report published in Feb.' 84 Impact, newsletter of the London group of Survival International, on the violation of human rights and civil liberties in the Chittagong Hill Trarcts in Bangladesh).

Impact

NEWSLETTER OF THE LONDON GROUP OF SURVIVAL INTERNATIONAL

NO. 4 FEB 1984

DEVELOPMENT FOR WHOM?

Bangladesh

An extraordinary state of affairs is prevailing in the Chittagong Hill Tracts. The Bangladesh Government has been carrying out a programme of systematic extermination of the indigenous nationalities of the Chittagong Hill Tracts because they are ethnically, religiously and culturaly different from the Muslim Bengalis. As a result, all human rights and civil liberties have been violated; tens of thousands of innocent tribal men, women and children have been murdered ; 12-15 thousand tribal people have been detained without trial, tortured and some of them killed, thousands of tribal women have been kidnapped, raped and many of them forcibly converted to Islam; tens of thousands of tribal farmers have been herded into concentration camps and their farm lands have been distributed among the outsider Muslim Bengalis ; about 852 of the tribal houses have been burnt ; the Buddhist temples have been desecrated and destroyed ; the Buddhist monks have been detained without trial, tortured and some of them killed ; and hundreds of thousands of outsider Muslim Bengalis have been rehabilitated by displacing the tribal farmers.

'Development' Bad For Tribals

In 1947, the tribal popualtion and Muslim Bengalis formed 98% and less than 2% respectively of the total population of the Chittagong Hill Tracts. By 1982, the Muslim Bengalis accounted for more than 50% of the population. All development works have created job oppurtunities for Muslim Bengalis only. The tribal people are not allowed to do business. During the colonial period the people of the Chittagong Hill Tracts enjoyed relative prosperity and employment, a certain degree of autonomy, rule of law and justice, and police and official protection whereas under the Muslim Bengali rule they have been deprived of all human rights and forced to become landless, jobless refugees. They are facing the prospect of total extinction.

ANNEXURE—VI

(Extract from the reports appearing in the Buddhist Peace Fellowship Newsletter, vol. 7, No 2 1985, in connection with the religious persecution of the Buddhists minority people in Bangladesh.)

BUDDHIST PEACE FELLOWSHIP, P. O. BOX 4650, BERKELEY, CA 94704, U. S. A.

Buddhist Peace Fellowship Newsletter
Volume 7, No. 2 1985

Tribal Buddhists Struggle For Life in Bangladesh

By Nelson Foster

Nearly five years ago, a Buddhist monk from the Chittagong Hill Tracts brought word to BPF of his people's heavy suffering — a suffering unknown to any of us at that time and still unknown, probably, to most of us. The situation of these tribal Buddhists has worsened over the intervening years, and it seems time to ask ourselves again what we can do to help.

The Hill Tracts, in southeastern Bangladesh, are the historic refuge of 12 tribes that are ethnically, culturally, and religiously different from the Bengali Muslim majority. Their lands, once regarded as marginal, have become attractive due to the nation's intense population pressures, and the tribal people—scorned as inferior—are being driven off in favor of Bengalis brought from other parts of Bangladesh.

In a report published last year, Survival International criticized Bangladesh govrnment for waging "a campaign of violence that in the past decade and a half has reached genocidal proportions."

A recent letter from the Hill Tracts concludes, "The government's declaration is: Either become Muslims or go away to other countries."

After BPF was alerted to the crisis in the Hill Tracts, board member Michael Roche a made a secret visit to the area and witnessed the plight of the tribal people firsthand. BPF began at that point a modest effort to bring this situation to the attention of relevant U. S. government agencies, human rights groups, and organizations such as the Asian Development Bank, which funnels most aid to Bangladesh. More recently, members of the British BPF have taken up the issue in a very active way.

At least two important human rights groups, the Anti-Slavery Society and Survival International, have now adopted oppression of the Hill tribes as a central concern. With the help of the Anti-Slavery Society, the Raiguru (Buddhist teacher of the king) of the Hill Tracts' largest tribe flew to Geneva last August to bring the issue before the U. N. Working Group on Indigenous Populations. The World Council of Indigenous Peoples has also taken an interest and BPF is now helping them gather information on which to act. BPF members are urged to educate themselves about conditions in the Hill Tracts. We recommend the Anti-Slavery Society's booklet *The Chittagong Hill Tracts : Militarization, oppression and the hill tribes*, avaliable for $ 5 from Third World Publications, 151 Stratford Rd., Birmingham BII IRD, U.K.

Politely worded letters of concern should be directed to General H. M. Ershad, President of the Republic of Bangladesh, Banga Bhawa, Dhaka, Bangladesh and to the Asian Development Bank, Roxas Boulevard, Manila, The Philippines. Letters to the ADB should ask that aid projects in the Hill Tracts be discontinued until such time as impartial observers can visit the projects and confirm that they benefit the tribal people.

Buddhist Peace Fellowship
Statement of purpose

*To make clear public witness to the Buddha Way as a way of peace and protection of all beings.

*To raise peace and ecology concerns among American Buddhists and to promote projects through which the Sangha may respond to these concerns.

*To encourage the delineation in English of the Buddhist way of non-violence, building from the rich resources of tradition Buddhist teachings a foundation for new action.

*To offer avenues to realize the kinship among groups and members of the American and world Sangha

*To serve as liaison to and enlist support for, existing national and international Buddhist peace and ecology programs.

*To provide a focus for concerns over the persecution of Buddhists as a particular expression of our intent to project all beings : and

*To bring the Buddhist perspective to contemporary peace and ecology movements.

Hatred is never appeased by hatred in this world ; it is appeased y love. This is eternal law.

Dbammapada

THE BUDDHIST PEACE FELLOWSHIP

By Michael Roche

In July the BPF board of directors made official response to the mesange brought in April by a brave emissary from Bangladesh : it adopted the task of allevinting the plight of the peoples of the Chittagong Hill Tracts as its first major project. In doing so, our young organization becam one of the few concerned groups standing between some 600,000 tribal people and what appears to be certain genocide.

Briefly, the tribespeople of Chittagong Hill Tracts are culturally and ethnically distinct in Bangladesh. Having maintained a tradition of Theravada Buddhism since the 15th century, they constitute an island of Buddhists in a sea of Muslim hostility.

There longterm isolation from the mainstream of S. E. Asian Buddhist history makes them a unique cultural ethnic entity and for that reason they have been studied by such western anthropologists as Claude Levi-Strauss. Even the British colonizers recognized this cultural uniqueness and, in 1900, instituted the Chittagong Hill Tracts Regulation, making the Hill Tracts area largely autonomous. This regulation has not since been officially abrogated, even by the present government of Bangladesh.

Since the 1960's, the Muslim majority of what is now Bangladesh has escalated efforts to appropriate the Hill Tracts and to destroy the tribal culture. With the Kaptai dam project, located squarely in the Hill Tracts, they flooded 350 square miles and displaced upwards of 100,000 tribespeople. This project employed no native people and has supplied them with virtually no electricity.

The harrassment of the 1960's did not end when, in 1972, the Bangladesh indepedence movement succeeded. Tribal people had aided in the independence effort hoping that the new regime would respect their cultural and territorial heritage. But soon after independence, the persecution began a new, as the government sought to consolidate its authority. An effort led by a member of Parliament to ask the government to respect the Chittagong Hill Tract Regulation of 1900 was answered by charges of secessionism, massive bloody reprisals and the burning of hundreds of villages. In response, the tribal people organized the Shanti Bahini or "Peace Force" to resist the government oppression.

Encountering this resistance and realizing that the tribal people weren't going to go quietly, the government has taken a new course, designed to conceal its ongoing repressive actions under the guise of "regional development". The Chittagong Hill Tracts Development Board founded in 1975, provides cover to the poverty-plagued government needs to continue attracting economic aid from liberal Western governments such as the United States Australia, and Federal Republic of Germany.

The Bangladesh government konws that if its actions are seen as the repression they are, vital international funds will be jeopardized. Withdrawal of aid has already occurred in the case of Sweden, which is pulling out of a program to "develop" timber resources in the Hill Tracts.

Thus, the Bangladesh authorities have recently adopted further tactics of obfuscation and deception. On the pretext of "rebel" violence, the government has sealed off the Hill Tracts so tightly that even U. S. State Dept. representatives are forbidden access. A ban has been placed on travel by the Hill people, and news is thoroughly censored.

A first step to dispel ignorance of the situation in Chittagong Hill Tracts was taken jointly by the International Fellowship of Reconciliation and BPF last spring, as they sponsored the international tour of a tribal representative. Contacting leaders of the nations supplying aid as well as members of the United nations, the speaker – unnamed for reasons of his safety – graphically described the plight of the tribespeople.

Information from this tour has been consolidated and updated by Ulrich Henes in an excellent article in IFOR Report. Titled "The Secret War in Bangladesh," this article is available from the BPF office in Berkeley.

A second step in this project, again jointly taken by BPF members and interested friends such as Mike Gabel of IFOR, has been follow-up contact with the State Department and members of Congress, asking use of America's aid-generated influence to persuade the Bangladesh authorities to reverse their course in the Hill Tracts.

To date, this second phase has achieved only mixed results Sen Charles Percy, soon to chair the Senate Foreign Relations Committee, has taken active interest in alleviating the situation in the Hill Tracts, and several other members of Congress express similar intent.

But all are hampered by a paucity of documentation and the Department of State's apparent desire to steer clear of controversy. The administration position, repeated with a dismaying regularity both to BPF members and interested Congressmen, can be summarized as follows: Since the Chittagong Hill Tract people are ethnically and religiously different from the people of lower Bangladesh, and since there is a greater density of population in the lowlands, the government opened the Hill Tracts for settlement in order to make opportunities equal and to put valuable resources to use.

This policy, if in fact it can be called a policy, has no moral or legal defence and is comparable to the violent plundering of land belonging to Native Americans. The State Department, however, seems to accept at face value both the Bangladesh government's "development" concern and its claim that the violence in the area has originated with the tribespeople. The Dacca government insists that it has made conciliatory gestures to the tribespeople and that it has cancelled the resettlement program, despite mounting evidence to the contrary.

The next phase in the Chittagong Hill Tracts project must be to dispel the cloud of ignorance and secrecy which surrounds the Hill Tracts. To this end, under joint sponsorship of BPF and IFOR, I'll visit Bangladesh next spring. My itinerary there is problematic, as the country is essentially a police state and travel is extremely restricted even outside the Hill Tracts. It should be possible, however, to reach members of Parliament who have spoken against the atrocities in the Hill Tracts and also to the American ambassador. It may be possible as well to interview tribespeople who no longer reside in the Hill Tracts.

Parliament turns disorderly

DACCA. Bangladesh—Parliament degenerated into a melee yesterday during protest, against, shoot to kill bill.

Opposition lawmakers disrupted proceedings with shouting and some legislators even broke microphones. Young opposition parliamentarians came close to exchanging blows with government offlcial. And some opposition lawmakers manhandled a government minister in the chamber.

Outside the building, baton-winging police battled demonstralors oppossing the blll.

The above report (*Honolulu Advertiser*, 12–11–80) may indicate a serious deterioration in the situation of the Hill Tracts people.

ANNEXURE – VII

(Letter to the President of Bangladesh, General H.M. Ershad from the Survival International, London,)

Survival International

For the rights of threatened tribal peoples

A Registered Charity No. 267444

29 Craven Street, London, WC2N 5NT, England.

Telephone : 01-839 3267

President : Robin Hanbury-Tenison, O.B.E.

Company Registration No. 1056317 Girobank No. 5664454

U.N. (ECOSOC)-N.G.O. EEC-NGO

General H.M. Ershad
President Republic of Bangladesh
Banga Bhawan Dhaka
Bangladesh.

12.7.1984

Dear President,

We wrote to you last year (14.4. 1983) concerning the grave situation of the tribal peoples in the Chittagong Hill Tracts (CHT), in the southeast of your country.

Since then we have received numerous further reports that indicate that the situation in the CHT remains critical and that serious human rights violations continue to be perpetrated by government forces and government-supported settlers. The details are presented in the accompanying report.

While on the one hand we welcomed the offer of amnesty made by your government to members of the *Shanti Bahini* in the early part of this year, we consider this move to be a totally inadequate response to the situation. It is only by going to meet the demands of the traditional peoples of the CHT that there can be any hope of achieving long term solutions to the problems of that area. Among the demands that we fully endorse are their claims for territorial security, a measure of self-determination and the retention of the Chittagong Hill Tracts Regulation of 1900.

We note with grave regret that your government continues to obfuscate and deny the existence of the serious problems in the CHT. For examble, Mr. Alimul Haque's response, to the Anti-Slavery' society detailed and well-documented allegations of gross human rights abuse by government forces in the CHT, presented to the Working Group on Indigenous Populations of the United Nations last year, should be a subject of shame for your government. Moreover the duplicity of the response of your representative Mr. Zamir, of the Bangladesh High Commission in London, is also reprehensible. In his meetings with delegates of the Scientific Buddhists Association, he alleged that members of OXFAM and Save the Children were helping to develop the arts and crafts of the tribal peoples of the area. In fact, as we have been able to verify, neither OXFAM nor OXFAM TRADING nor the Save the Childern Fund (UK), nor the Save the Children Foundation (USA) have any operations among the tribals of the CHT. It is inexcusable that the good name of these organisations be used to cover up the genocidal abuse of tribal peoples' rights.

We urge that you give these matters your immediate attention and look forward to hearing how you plan to resolve the problems.

Yours sincerely
(Sd)
Robin Hanbury-Tenison
President

ANNEXURE-VIII

(A report of Survival International Information Pack on the escalation of violence and seizure of tribal land in CHT.)

SURVIVAL INTERNATIONAL–INFORMATION PACK–UPDATE
CHITTAGONG HILL TRACTS : BANGLADESH

Escalating violence and the seizure of tribal land, supported by the Bangladeshi army, is affecting 400,000 tribal people of 13 ethnic groups in the Chittagong Hill Tracts (CHT) area of Bangladesh. The CHT peoples are a predominantly Buddhist population (others are Christian, Hindu or have their own religion) which is racially and culturally distinct from the predominantly Muslim Bengali population of Bangladesh.

Since the Information Pack was first issued in May 1981, the situation in this area has deteriorated. Civilian observers are banned from the region, but reports from the area say that important army operations have taken place in which hundreds of tribal people have been killed and many have been tortured, raped and otherwise mistreated. Tens of thousands of these people have been driven from their homelands.

In June 1981, a local member of parliament, Upendra Lal Chakma, called a press conference in Dacca to report a new wave of attacks on tribal people (in Matiranga district) by Bengali settlers and military personnel. This was the second attempt by the MP to bring attention to the abuses being perpetrated. It was Upendra Lal Chakma, and other MPs, who reported the Kalampati massacres in May 1980. At that time, the Home Minister of Bangladesh was obliged to call an official enquiry into the Kalampati incident. This enquiry has never reported.

During 1981 conditions continued to deteriorate. Between Septemper and December of that year some 20,000 tribal people fled from the Bangladeshi army across the border into India. Many more were turned back by both Bangladeshi and Indian border guards. These refugees reported full-scale military attacks upon them in conjunction with attacks by lowland settlers.

Tne refugees were a cause of tension between the two countries. After several months in the Indian State of Tripura, the UN High Commission for refugees was eventually able to negotiate the peoples' return to Bangladesh. But on their return, it is claimed that many found their lands already occupied by Bengalis. These reports suggest that these people are now landless and destitute.

The deterioration in the CHT reflects a major shift in the national situation in Bangladesh. In 1981, the then President, Gen. Ziaur Rahman, was assassinated in an attempted coup involving Gen. Manzoor, the officer in charge of military operations in the CHT,. The coup attempt failed and Gen. Manzoor and several other offcers were killed.

In the wake of the attempted coup, the army has strengthened its hold on the country, deposing an elected President and replacing him with Gen. H.M. Ershad who now controls the country with the aid of special Martial Law powers. The military has also purged its own ranks. Many officers who were politically active within the army in support of the Bangladesh independence movement during the early 1970s have been replaced. Those now in control come generally from the ranks of professional soldiers who were serving in Pakistan at the time of the independence struggle. They are characterised as the more conservative and hardline elements. If former Gen. Manzoor made some tentative attempts to negotiate with the tribal people, represented by their organisation, the Shanti Bahini, the present leadership seems even more intent than before on a military solution to the CHT problem.

which threatens the lives and culture of hundreds of thousands of tribal people.

Bangladesh is a predominantly Muslim country and so the independent traditions of Buddhism, Christianity and Hinduism which prosper in the CHT have always been a point of tension. Pakistan, including present day Bangladesh, was created by the British largely on the basis of its Muslim religious unity. Muslim Bengalis remain suspicious of the loyalties of the non-Muslim tribes. For their part, the peoples of the CHT are most fearful of forced assimilation. The speculation by Gen. Ershad during January 1983 that the country might become an Islamic state is, therefore, an issue of grave concern for the peoples of the CHT and a further sign of government intolerance.

Concern at the deteriorating situation has been indicated in two major international withdrawals from development projects in the region. In May 1981, we reported that the Swedish International Development Authority had withdrawn its cooperation from a forestry project in the CHT. More recently, the Australian Overseas Development Agency has terminated its contract and withdrawn personnel from a road construction programme which has been widely criticised for its destructive effects. Local people see this programme as primarily to the advantage of the Bangladeshi army in moving troops into the region. It is also a major access route for Bengali settlers. It is along the road where settlers are easily supported by the army that much of the land siezure and violence has occurred.

Despite these decisions reflecting international concern even at governmental level, others have continued to cooperate with Bangladeshi government activities in the area. Prominent among these collaborators is the Asia Development Bank which is involved in a 48 million dollar CHT development project which includes road construction, the development of infrastructure and support for the development of commercial farming in the CHT. Under present circumstances such projects seem destined to assist and attract further Bengali encroachment into tribal lands which, in turn, will lead to more violence and the rapid destruction of tribal culture. It is important that pressure be brought on the Asia Development Bank to suspend this project because of the present situation and in the light of the actions of other experienced development agencies.

Recipients of this Information Pack are, therefore, urged to protest this situation by writing their own letters, similar to the ones attached, in their own name to :

Asia Development Bank
Roxas Boulevard
Manila
Philippinnes

General H.M. Ershad
President of the Republic
of Bangladesh
Banga Bhawan Dacca
Bangladesh

ANNEXURE – IX

(Letter to the President Ziaur Rahman of Bangladesh from Holland based International Fellowship of Reconciliation regretting the violation of minority rights in CHT.)

INTERNATIONAL FELLOWSHIP OF RECONCILIATION

Holvan Sonoy 15-17 | 1811 LD Alkmaar Holland
Phone 072-123014

20 February 1981

President Ziaur Rahman

President's Secretariat

Bongo Bhaban

Dacca

Bangladesh

Dear President Rahman,

It is only a month before the people of Bangladesh celebrate the 10 years of independence, which is not so long a time that people in the rest of the world have forgotten the torture and cruelty suffered in Bangladesh in the struggle for independence.

Because of world attention to that suffering, and horror with the methods used by the opposing military forces, Bangladesh was founded with the world's applause and a great reservoir of good will. One expression of this support was the substantial aid from other countries for reconstruction and development.

Unfortunately, policies of the government of Bangladesh in regard to the Chittagong Hill Tracts are increasingly coming to world attention and are deeply shaking the foundations of respect and support for Bangladesh.

The tribal peoples in the Chittangong Hill Tracts region form a small minority among the Bengali people. Even should many of them turn from the peaceableness for which they are renowned and seek in violence a way to protect their lands and culture, ultimately they are quite defenseless against the military forces which can be raised against them.

Adding to the dismay and alarm felt by many longtime supporters of Bangladesh is the government's recent introduction to the Parliament of thc proposed Disturbed Area Bill, which would allow police and military personnel to shoot and kill any person within a "distrubed area", to arrest without warrant, to search homes without judicial permit, to destroy homes merely on the suspicion that they were used for the storage of weapons or explosives, and to confiscate personal property.

In seeking such appalling legislation, the government really confesses to the most shocking charges that are being lodged against it by the people of the Chittagong Hill Tracts, who testify to summary killings, torture, arrest and detainment without charges, harassment, and the widescale destruction not only of homes but of entire villages.

How disturbing it is should we learn that minority rights were better guarded there in the imperialist period than under self rule.

Mister President, we appeal as a non-aligned movement with members throughout the world that the Disturbed Area Act be withdrawn and that the government take urgent steps to assure the human rights of the minority peoples, including land tenure as well as political and cultural rights.

Most sincerely,
(Sd)
James H. Forest.
Coordinator

ANNEXURE – X

(Letter to General H.M. Ershad, President of Bangladesh from Survival International on the violation of the tribal peoples' rights in CHT.)

Survival International

(Primitive Peoples' Fund) Limited
A Registered Charity No. 267444
36 Craven street, London WC2N 5NG, England
Telephone : 01-839 3267

Director : Barbara Bentley President : Robin Handbury-Tenison, O.B.E.

Company Registration No. 1056317 Girobank No. 5664454
U.N. (Ecosoc) N.G.O. EEC-NGO

General H.M. Ershad
President of the Republic of Bangladesh
Banga Bhawan, Dacca
Bangladesh

14 April 1983

Dear President,

We have received alarming reports that the situation of the tribal peoples in the Chittagong Hill Tracts area of Bangladesh has deteriorated over recent years. These reports indicate that tens of thousands of these peoples have been forced to leave their homelands and that many others have been killed and abused by the Bangladeshi army.

In the light of this situation, we urge you to take immediate action to defend the lives, land and rights to religious and cultural freedom of the tribal people of the Chittagong Hills.

We also urge you to end government aid to newly settled non-tribal immigrants in the area and to put a stop to this immigration which entails the violation of the tribal peoples' rights.

We are particularly alarmed at the role the Bangladeshi army is taking in this situation through its consitent and brutal violations of tribal peoples' rights, and we urge you to give this matter your immediate attention.

We suggest that the area be opened to impartial observers to visit and report on the situation there.

We are publishing copies of this letter on an internationa level and will, similarly, publish any replies we may receive to it.

Yours sincerely,
(Sd)
Barbara Bentley
Director

ANNEXURE–XI

(Reports to the United Nations Working Group on Indigenous populations about attacks on tribespeople in CHT)

ANTI-SLAVERY SOCIETY
for the
PROTECTION OF HUMAN RIGHTS
Report for 1985
to the
United Nations working Group on Indigenous Populations

Bangladesh : Chittagong Hill Tracts—attacks on the Chakma and other tribes

Since 1981 the Anti-Slavery Society has regularly reported its concern over the incursions by Bengali settlers into the Chittagong Hill Tracts (CHT) a region protected until 1964 by the Chittagong Hill Tracts Regulation of 1900. The purpose of the Regulation and subsequent legislation was to protect the tribal peoples of the region, to enable them to maintain their distinctive way of life and to safeguard their cultural and religious beliefs.

Following the Kaokhali Massacre of 25 March 1980 when an estimated 300 tribal people were massacred by elements of the Bangladeshi army. Mr. Upendra Lal Chakma the Member of Parliament representing the Chittagong Hill Tracts, called for a Parliamentary enquiry to establish the facts and to identify those responsible for the massacre. A five-man Parliamentary Committee headed by the then Home Minister, Mr. Mustafizar Rahman was in fact appointed but so far no investigation of this indefensible massacre has taken place.

Now further detailed evidence has come into the hands of the Anti-Slavery Society regarding a series of grossly violent attacks on tribal communities which took place between 12 April 1984 and 15 February 1985. The details are tragically familiar : rape, murder and arson are the triple themes which run through this very explicit evidence.

The working Group on Indigenous Populations is primarily concerned with the setting of standards and in reply to a previous intervention by the Anti-Slavery Society, the Bangladesh Government's representative Mr. Ahmed Hoque declared on 12 August 1983 that the Society's report could not be seen as "a *bona fide* contribution to a scientific study aimed at the primary objective of this working group, namely the evolution of standards regarding the rights of Indigenous Peoples."

With the utmost respect the Anti-Slavery Society would like to remark that standards are drawn up in order to be applied and applied to the conditions of living human beings. Without evidence of the effect of the application or non-application of these standards the whole process would seem to be pointless.

The 325 individual cases described in the attached appendix are therefore to be regarded not simply as cases of gross violations of human rights in general, but quite specifically as evidence of the urgent need to proceed with the setting of standards and the equally urgent need to provide the national and international machinery to ensure their implementation.

The fact of the matter is that the Chakma people and the other 12 hill tribes, are faced with the prospect of genocide if the present violent actions against them are permitted to continue. Great hopes were raised when General Ershad on his elevation to the Presidency of Bangladesh in 1983 offered amnesty to the Shanti Bahini, the tribal resistance force. Unfortunately there seems to have been little change and the events reported in the appendix differ only in detail from those reported at the time of the Kaokhali Massacre of 1980.

The Anti-Slavery Society has the greatest sympathy with the demands of the indigenous peoples of the Chittagong Hill Tracts for self-determination and autonomy, for the release of tribal people now in prison and for cessation of settlement by non-tribal Bengalis from outside the region. As a first step, however, the Society proposes that a Special Rapporteur be appointed to enquire into the present situation in the Chittagong Hill Trácts and to make recommendations as to measures to be taken to restore peace to the region, to ensure the continuance of the tribal peoples way of life and culture and for the harmonious development of the area in the best interests of its inhabitants, The Special Rapporteur should be invited to report if possible to the Commission on Human Rights at its forty second-ession in February 1986; failing this he should report to the thirty eighth Session of the Sub-Commission on Prevention of Discrimination and Protection of Minorities in August 1986.

My appeal to the united nations working group on indigenous Populations

I, being a victim of the Bangladesh regime's inhuman oppression in the Chittagong Hill Tracts (CHT), would like to present my appeal for help to the Human Rights Commission.

The CHT is a tribal area of 5093 square miles in the south-eastern corner of Bangladesh bordering India and Burma. It is the traditional home of 12 tribes about 600,000 in all. They are ethnically mongoloid, culturally close to the ethnic groups of Burma and eastern India, and religiously Buddhists, Hindus and Christians. Because of their different culture, religion and ethnic origin the tribal people have suffered extreme hostility from the neighbouring Bengalis for centuries.

Britain recognised the difficult situation of the tribal people and creatsed an autonomous area, the Chittagong Hill Tracts, exclusively for the tribal people and administered it under the *CHT Regulation of* 1900. This required that all govt. functionaries apart from a few British high officials be recruited locally. There was a separate police establishment called the *CHT Police* which was mostly manned by tribal people except the Superintendent of Police who was British. Non-tribal people were not allowed to settle in the district permanently, nor could they purchase land from the tribal people. Under Rule 51 they could be expelled from the district if they were undesirable or found doing anything prejudicial to the interest of the tribal people. In short, this Regulation protected the political, economic, social and religious rights of the people of the CHT.

Schools, hospitals, surveying, road-building, postal and telegraph services, courts, mechanised boats, water works, electricity, modern administration, rule of law and justice and so on were first introduced during the British period. The majority of the tribal people possessed flat farming land in the valleys. They had developed the farming lands themselves and practised plough cultivation. The tribal people who did not possess flat farming land cultivated the hill slopes by the slash-and-burn cultivation method (*Jhum*).

After independence in 1947, Sir Cyril Radcliffe, the Chairman of the Boundary Commission awarded the CHT to Pakistan although 98 per cent of the poulation of the CHT were non-Muslims at the time of independence. The inclusion of the CHT into Pakistan was bitterly resented by the tribal people. Under the Pakistani rule the CHT Regulation of 1900 was left standing but its rules were not observed. Bengali officers and settlers were brought in, the tribal police force was disbanded and its officers together wtih other tribal civilian officers were transferred to other districts of East Pakistan. The Bengalis even interfered with the social and religious life of the people of the CHT. For example, in 1953, the Chakma Chief *Raja Tridiv Roy*, was mobbed by the Government-backed Bengalis while administering justice in his Royal Court in his capacity as a magistrate. In spite of the personal intervention of the then British Deputy Commissioner, *Lt. Col. John Angus Hume* OBE, he was arrested and humiliated by the Bengali police. The Chakma Chief fulfils a role similar to that of the

British Constitutional Monarchy. He Would have been killed without the intervention of Col. Hume. This highly admired British officer protested against this gross injustice by resigning his post.

Large-scale Muslim Bengali settlement on the farming lands of the tribal farmers resulted in the eviction of about 100,000 tribespeople. The largest single eviction of 60,000 took place in 1961 when Bengali immigrants started a series of riots against the tribal farmers. The riots were stopped only when the Indian, Sri Lankan and other Governments lodged protest with the Pakistani regime. The evicted tribals were pushed into India and Burma and none of them was repatriated, The US-financed Hydro-electric Dam on the Karnafuli river at Kaptai submerged 350 square miles of low land including 40 per cent of the best farming land of the CHT and uprooted more than 100,000 tribal farmers. The Government took no effective steps to rehabilitate them or to compensate them adequately. Many tribals died during the removal and many fled to the Indian States of Tripura and Mizoram. The project has not employed any tribal people and has supplied them with virtually no electricity. Other economic benefits such as fish farming and industries have also been exclusively allotted to the Bengalis. Tribal farming lands were acquired by the Government to set up a paper mill and a rayon mill at Chandraghona and also other industries in the district. Only a few tribal people have been employed there. During the 24 years of Pakistani rule the tribal people lost practically all their political, economic and social rights including official and police protection.

During the 1971 war for independence of Bangladesh most tribal people sided with Bangladeshi forces in the hope that under independence their condition would improve. But when the Pakistani forces withdrew from the CHT, hundreds of tribal people were killed and their villages destroyed by the Bangladesh Mukti Bahini. Soon after independence, *Sheikh MujiburRahman* sent his armed forces to massacre the tribal people. Shaken by these attacks the tribal people sent a delegation under the leadership of *Manabendra narayan larma* to Sheikh

Mujib asking for autonomy and enforcement of the CHT Regulation of 1900. He rejected their demands and said "Do away with your ethnic identity, go home and be Bengalis". Then he resorted to more violence and allowed more Bengali immigration. After the Government's rejection of all peaceful methods of resolving the CHT crisis the tribal people had no other alternative but to organise the "Shanti Bahini" or "Peace Force" with a view to resisting the Government oppression. During the civil war and after independence tens of thousands of Bengalis forcibly occupied tribal farming lands.

After the assassination of Sheikh Mujib, a tribal delegation submitted a memorandum to the President of Bangladesh, *Justice A. S. Sayem*, demanding regional autonomy. Again similar proposals were made to President *Ziaur Rahman*. The successive Governments of Bangladesh responded to their requests by intensifying repression. As a result all civil liberties and human rights have been violated. Tens of thousands of innocent tribal people have been murdered; 12-15 thousand tribals have been detained without trial and tortured; thousands of tribal women have been kidnapped, raped and forcibly converted to Islam; hundreds of villages have been burnt; hundreds of Buddhist temples have been desecrated and destroyed and hundreds of monks have been tortured and killed; tens of thousands of tribal farmers have been forcibly moved to concentration camps and their farming lands and villages have been distributed among the Bengali settlers. The Government provided them with free transport, food, money, land and protection. The settlers harass the tribal people, take their stock, rape their women, burn their villages and start riots. When the tribals complain to the army and police, no action is taken. Eventually the trible people just move out. By 1982, over half a million Bengalis had been settled by expelling tribal farmers.

During the British period a tribal family could hold 25 acres of farming land. The Pakistani Government reduced the land holding ceiling to 10 acres and the Bangladeshi regime has reduced it further to 5 acres. This law has never been applied to any parts of Bangladesh except the CHT. On the other hand, the Muslim Bengalis can hold unlimitted land. Even the present *Land reforms Committee* has recommended fixing the land holding ceiling for each family at 25-33 acres. Now the army is compelling the tribal farmers to surrender their lands to accommodate the Bengalis. Those who try to protest are summarily driven out or taken to army camps where they are detained in pits.

As a result of military campaigns thousands of tribal families have taken shelter in the forest and have been living on roots and leaves. They could not return to their home because their villages have already been occupied by the settlers. Many tribals and the children died of starvation. There is a serious shortage of essential commodities such as salt, rice, kerosene, cloth and medicine due to the Government's restriction on their movement. The tribal people are not allowed to buy more than two kilograms of rice per family per week. A family has normally six members and this amount of food is totally inadequate for six people and most of the tribal people suffer from lack of food. The tribal people require special permits to carry medicine and to get such a permit a tribal must go to government centres which are usually miles away from their villages. On the way there are military and police checkposts where the tribals are harassed, tortured and detained in pits without food and water, and women are raped. In effect, the tribal people are being deprived of medicine and other daily necessities. As a consequence a large number of tribal people are dying of malaria and of other diseases. The Bangladeshi regime is adopting every means to get rid of the people of the CHT. All tribal people must always carry identity cards and they are not permitted to own businesses. The Bangladesh Government has been covering up its genocidal crimes and it does not allow foreign and local journalists to visit the interior.

The Bangladesh Government often seeks foreign aid for the economic and social development of the tribal people. After receiving the aid the Government uses the money for the military and the Bengali settlers and not for the tribal people. For example:

a. Sweden—(SIDA= Swedish International Development Agency) financed *Forest Development project* created job opportunities for the Bengalis only. Swedn stopped the project because the Bangladesh Government refused to employ the tribal people.

b. UNICEF (United Nations International Children's Emergency Fund)- sponsored *Drinking Water Supply scheme* benefited only army camps, Bengali colonies, urban centres and concentration camps.

c. WHO (World Health Organization) -organised *Malaria Eradication Project* has been mainly used to protect the armed forces and the Bengali settlers.

d. Asian Development Bank-assisted *Livestock and fisheries Programmes* has benefited the Bengali new comers.

e. Australia-aided *Chengi valley road Building project* has been used to facilitate army movement in the hills and to open up the interior to the Bengali immjgration.

The tribal people welcome foreign aid if it is used for their benefit. But at present foreign aid is helping the Bengalis only. So they have appealed to the donor countries to stop their aid to Bangladesh, because this aid is being used to annihilate the tribal people.

The indigenous people of the CHT are facing the prospect of extinction. They need the protection of the international community since the Bangladeshi regime does not speak the language of justice, humanity and tolerance. In view of the extreme hostility of the Bangladesh Government I suggest the following measures to ensure the survival of the tribal people.

1. Immediate release of all tribal people imprisoned in jails and detention centres in different parts of Bangladesh.
2. Immediate removal of all non-tribal settlers from the CHT.
3. Immediate withdrawal of all Bangladesh armed forces including the non-tribal police force from the CHT.
4. Retention of the CHT Regulation of 1900 and constitutional provision restricting the amendment of the Regulation.
5. Autonomy for the Chittagong Hill Tracts with its own legislature and recognition of the tribal people's right to self determination.

6. Deployment of the United Nations peace keeping force in the CHT and implementation of the said operations under the auspices of the UNO.

I extend my thanks to those who helped me and offered me this opportunity to tell the sad stories of suffering in my homeland, the Chittagong Hill Tracts. Thank you all.

'Sabbe Satta Sukhita Bhabantu'
'Let all living beings be happy'

Yours sincerely
Sd/-
A.V. Mahathero
Rajguru

Dated 1.8.84

UNITED NATIONS
ECONOMIC AND SOCIAL COUNCIL
COMMISSION ON HUMAN RIGHTS
Sub-Commission on Prevention of
Discrimination and Protection of Minorities
Working Group on Indigenous Populations

Geneva 29 July—2 August 1985

Statement submitted by Ven. Aggavansa Mahathera on behalf of the people of the Chittagong Hill Tracts.

Madam Chairman,

I, Aggavansa Mahathera, a Chakma Buddhist monk from the Chittagong Hill Tracts (CHT), Bangladesh, would like to draw the attention of the Members of the Working Group to the precarious situation of the indigenous people of the CHT.

All successive rulers of Bangladesh have unleashed a reign of terror in the CHT, the traditional homeland of 13 mongoloid tribes who profess Buddhism, Hinduism and Christianity, and cultivate Tibeto-Burman culture. However, conditions for the indigenous people have worsened since Gen. Hossain Mohammad Ershad has seized power by overthrowing the elected Government of President Abdus Sattar. The present military regime is persecuting the tribal people more ruthlessly than its predecessors. It has sealed off the area and deployed over 125,C00 military and para-military personnel, one unit of the Bangladesh navy and the entire Bangladesh air force to exterminate the local people systematically on the one hand and to settle over half a million outsider Bengalis in their place on the other. As a result of the government-directed violence about 185,000 tribal men, women and children died and the pogrom is continuing unabated.

On 31 May 1984, the members of the Bangladesh army and the Bengali settlers mounted a series of attacks on the tribal villages—Ludibash Chara, Ujyang Chari, Suguri Para, Het Bharia, Gorasthan, Bhushan Chara, Garjan Tali and Dhanu Bak—within Barkal Thana, resulting in 69 deaths. Most of the victims were women and children and they were murdered most brutally. For example:

1. Mrs. Sneha Bala Chakma, 35, wife of Mr. Mohan Chakma of Suguri Para, was raped by many attackers. She was bleeding profusely. Then she and her 1 year old son, Nanda Kumar Chakma, were killed with bayonet charges.

2. Mrs. Nila Mukhi Chakma, 33, wife of Mr. Boli Mohan Chakma of Suguri Para, was raped by many invaders. She was bleeding profusely. Then the soldiers charged her with bayonets through the bleeding private parts of her body and shot her in the breasts.

3. Miss Chaya Rani Chakma, 14, daughter of Mr. Dalam Chakma of Suguri Para, was raped by many soldiers. She was bleeding profusely. Then she and her mother were thrown into the fire.

The Buddhist temples were looted and the monks were beaten severely. Some 5,000 tribal people sought refuge in the Indian State of Mizoram and about 10,000 fled into the surrounding forests.

On 30 June 1984, the Bengali settlers were prompted by the Bangladesh army to forcibly reap the Chakma' rice crops. When the tribals resisted, the Bengali soldiers emerged from concealment and launched attacks on several tribal villages named as Chota Harina, Bara Harina, Chedoa, Garjan Tali,

Suguri Para and Maudong. More than 300 Chakmas were murdered. The captured tribals were divided into three groups—old and young men, elderly women, and young women. Men and old women were shot dead. The young Women were raped freely, some of them were killed and some were converted to Islam. Abcut 13,000 tribal refugees crossed into Mizoram State and many thousands of others took refuge in the adjacent forests.

About 4100 tribal refugees have been settled in two camps at Tibira Ghat and Tagalak Bak in Mizoram. The other refugees were pushed back to the CHT by the Mizoram Administration. They could not return to their villages because the Bengali settlers had already occupied them. Now these uprooted tribal people have taken refuge in the upland forests in the CHT. Their fate is not known. Survival International has reported that "the situation of the refugees currently resident in Mizoram State, India, is far from satisfactory". Many young and aged members of the group died due to meagre diet and scarcity of medicines.

Survival International has revealed that the Bangladesh army pursued a scorched earth policy in the Gaba Chari region in the Subalong valley mostly inhabited by the tribal slash-and-burn (Jhum) cultivators. During a month-long operation, between 20 September and 19 October 1984, the Bengali soldiers destroyed six villages, namely, Bar Kalak, Othyal Chara, Harin Hat Para, Mong chari, Shivram Para and Bamer Subalong. Houses were burnt, crops were destroyed, harvests were taken, and villagers were evicted from their ancestral homes. It is, perhaps, noteworthy that the 'scorched earth policy' has characterised the government's activities in the tribal homeland for many years.

On the orders of the highest authorities of Bangladesh, the Bengali soldiers and the Bengali settlers rape hundreds of tribal women everyday. For instance,

1 On 31 October 1984, Miss Chikonbi Chakma, 16, daughter of Mr. Padma Kumar Chakma of Kalabanya in Mahal Chari Thana, was raped by 4 Bengali soldiers in front of her father. Then she was taken to the local military camp.

She was not released despite her parents' request to the camp commander.

2. On 14 January 1985, the members of the Bangladesh Rifles of Dewan Para BDR camp surrounded the house of Mr. Shombu Nath Chakma of Dewan Para in Matiranga Thana and raped his daughter, Miss Jhurongini Chakma, 17.

In complicity with the Bangladesh security forces, the Bengali settlers occupy tribal lands forcibly. The tribal farmers are punished if they complain to the authorities against the Bengali intruders. For example:

1. A Bengali settler named Mohammad Ali built his house forcibly on the land of Mr. Dukhya Ram Chakma, 22, of Amtoli Adam in Merung Thana. On 31 December 1984, this Bengali set fire on his house and then complained to Lt. Hatem, a Bengali military officer of the Chongra Chari camp, that the local tribals burned his house. Lt. Hatem called the local tribal leader, Mr. Indrajoy Karbari, 58, and ordered him to pay Taka 10,000/- to the Bengali settler as compensation.

2. The Bengali settlers also forcibly occupied the land of Mr. Jugen Chakma, 44, of Chota Merung in Merung Thana. On 31 December 1984, the local tribal leaders—Mr. Guna Dhar Chakma, Mr. Hriday Ranjan Chakma, Mr. Surendra Chakma, Mr. Nihar Bindu Chakma and Mr. Bimal Kanti Chakma went to Merung police station to protest against the forcible occupation of tribal land. The Bengali Officer-in-Charge did not take any actions against the Bengalis. Instead he arrested these innocent tribal leaders on charges of arson and sent them to Khagrachari jail.

The root of the crisis in the CHT is that the government wants the land only for its co-religionists and not the people of the CHT because of their different race, religion and culture. The military regime is bent on solving the crisis simply by killing the indigenous people. Their survival is totally dependent on the help of the international community. I appeal fervently to you to take the following measures in order to protect the people of the CHT from the violent Bengali invasion.

1. Immediate release of all tribal people imprisoned in jails and detention centres in different parts of Bangladesh.
2. Immediate removal of all non-tribal settlers from the CHT.
3. Immediate withdrawal of all Bangladesh armed forces including the non-tribal police force from the CHT.
4. Retention of the Chittagong Hill Tracts Regulation of 1900 and constitutional provision restricting the amendment of the Regulation.
5. Autonomy for the Chittagong Hill Tracts with its own legislature and recognition of the Chittagong Hill Tracts People's right to self-determination.
6. Deployment of the United Nations peace keeping force in the CHT and supervision of the said operations under the auspices of the UNO.

Thank you for lending me your ears. I would like to express my deep gratitude to the Anti-Slavery Society for helping me to participate in this conference.

'Sabbe Satta Sukhita Bhabantu'
'Let All Living Beings Be Happy'

Aggavansa Mahathera
(Chakma Rajguru)

ANNEXURE—XII

(Report of Anti-Slavery Society for the Protection of Human Rights for 1984 to the United Nations Working Group on Indigenous Populations)

ANTI-SLAVERY SOCIEY FOR THE PROTECTION OF HUMAN RIGHTS

(A banned item until 1st August, 1984)

Report For 1984 to the

United Nations Working Group On Indigenous Populations

BANGLADESH

At last year's session of the Working Group on Indigenous Populations the Anti-Slavery Society drew the attention of the experts to the situation of the tribal minority peoples living in the Chittagong Hill Tracts of Bangladesh. In that submission we stated that numerous human rights violations were being perpetrated by the armed forces against the tribal peoples, including murder, torture and sacrilegious attacks on Buddhist monks and temples. A full report has now been completed and presented to the Human Rights Centre.

This year the Society wishes to address itself to the two matters under discussion during this session : the question of definition and of land. In the working definition proposed by the Special Rapporteur, Mr Martinez Cobo, indigenous Populations are described as "the existing descendants of the people who inhabited the present territory of a country at the time when persons of a different culture or ethnic origin arrived." In various submissions by indigenous peoples organizations, in Convention 107 of the International Labour Organisation, and implicitly in various United Nations instruments, it has been stated that these people have a right to their own land.

The distinguished representative of Bangladesh stated last year that Bangladesh had no indigenous peoples. He also stated that the Bengali-speaking majority had been settled in the area from prehistoric times. He maintained that the Working Group should be addressing itself to those situations such as Australasia where, and I quote, "a colonising and racially distinct people coming from overseas established settlement and entered into conflict with the autochthon pupulation."

The Chittagong Hill Tracts have been inhabited since time immemorial by hill tribes different in race, religion and culture from the Muslim Bengali majority of Bangladesh. They retained their autonomy during Mughal and British occupation of the region. Until the 1950s more than 90 per cent of the population was tribal. Bengalis from the plains have only begun to settle in the hill tracts in the last two decades.

When Bengalis came in small numbers they were always welcomed by the tribespeople but in recent years they have come in thousands; they arrive poor and unfamiliar with their new environment and completely unaware of the culture and traditions of the inhabitants of the region. They have no knowledge of the communal land base of the tribal communities, they have no skills in living in the forests and hills as shifting cultivators and they regard with suspicion and derision the clothing, way of life and customs of the tribespeople.

In the last decade the clashes between these two distinct cultures have led to at least two serious massacres of tribespeople : in 1980 at Kaokhali and in 1981 at Matiranga. The inhabitants of the hill tracts fear for their lives. Tribal villagers hide themselves when soldiers of the Bangladeshi army are reported in the vicinity such is the terror now prevalent in the tracts.

The Anti-Slavery Society is quite willing to take the situation in Australia as the paradigm for the work of these sessions, as the distinguished representative of Bangladesh urges. We know as well as any what happened to the aboriginal population of Australia in the first century of occupation. A population of 300,000 was reduced by 4/5ths and the aborigines were excluded from all but the most inhospitable areas of the country. The European settlers there did not acknowledge land held communally, just as in the hill tracts today land that is untitled is claimed as government land and disposed of accordingly. In the last two decades the indigenous peoples of the region have faced persistent land alienation. More than 100,000 tribespeople were displaced in the 1960s as the result of a hydro-electirc power project on the Karnaphuli River. The reservoir inundated 250 square miles and 40 per cent of the cultivable land of the Chittagong Hill Tracts. At no time was there consultation with the hill-people. Indeed, a study undertaken in 1979 discovered that 93 per cent of those affected believe that their economic condition has deteriorated as a consequence of that development.

Since the independance of Bangladesh in 1972 there has been a rapid growth of new settlements by non-tribal Bengalis from the plains. By 1981 it is estimated that nearly 200,000 had been settled. In July 1982, a new settlement programme was authorised by the Bangladeshi government by which a further quarter of a million Bengalis would be transferred to the district. This massive programme of settlement will make the indigenous peoples of the Chittagong Hill Tracts a minority in their own land.

The people of the hill tracts are not seeking independence, nor the creation of a separate state apart from Bangladesh, but the recognition that they have the right to their traditional way of life, their own land and some measure of control over their own development. The present situation of terror and violence cannot be allowed to continue. A new policy from the Bangladeshi government aimed at providing some tribal autonomy and guaranteeing rights is a necessity. The Anti-Slavery Society recommends most earnestly that the Government of Bangladesh :

(1) enter into discussion with all sectors of tribal society in the Chittagong Hill Tracts with a view to reaching a political settlement which would respect the land rights, future and identity of indigenous peoples;

(2) bring an immediate halt to the influx of settlers into the tracts;

(3) investigate human rights violations against tribal peoples in the hill tracts.

Finally, the Anti-Slavery Society urges the Government of Bangladesh to allow free access to the troubled region to international observers and journalists. This measure alone would do much to reduce the level of fear and suspicion felt by the tribespeople of the hill tracts.

* * *

News Release

Appeal to United Nations for Chittagong Hill Tracts Peoples

Geneva, August 7, 1984—"Without autonomy, there is no survival for the people of the Chittagong Hill Tracts" declared the Ven. Aggavansa Mahathero, a Buddhist monk in his appeal to the UN Working Group on Indigenous populations, the main UN body dealing with tribal peoples.

Ven. Aggavansa stressed the continuing violence against the tribal peoples. "As a result of military campaigns thousands of tribal families have taken shelter in the forest. Many tribals and their children have died of stravation. There is a serious shortage of essential commodities such as salt, rice, kerosene and medicine. The tribal people are being deprived of medicine and are dying of malaria and other diseases."

Ven. Aggavansa is the first person of the Chittagong Hill Tracts to address a UN body, and the Working Group listened with care as he described the efforts of the Bangladesh regime to settle new Bangali settlers in the Chittagong Hill Tracts at the expense of the Tribal populations. "The settlers harass the tribal people, take their stock, rape their woman, burn their villages and start riots. When the tribals complain to the army and the police no action is taken."

Ven. Aggavansa Mahathero, the Rajguru of the Chakma tribe is now in exile in India where he is active in informing world public opinion on the fate of the tribes of the Chittagong Hill Tracts as well as bringing spiritual help to Chittagong Hill people who have sought refuge in India.

In keeping with the Buddhist tradition of seeking peace, Ven. Aggavansa Mahathero called upon the Working Group to offer the protection of the international community to the people of the Chittagong Hill Tracts and called especially for :

(1) Immediate withdrawal of all Bangladesh armed forces including the non-tribal police force from the Chittagong Hill Tracts and their replacement by a United Nations peace-keeping force under the auspices of the United Nations.

(2) Immediate release of all tribal people imprisoned in jails and detention centres in different parts of Bangladesh.

(3) Autonomy for the Chittagong Hill Tracts with its own legislature and recognition of the tribal people's right to self-determination.

(4) Immediate removal of all non-trlbal settlers from the Chittagong Hill Tracts.

He indicated the willingness of the Chittagong Hill Tracts representatives to negotiate with the Bangladesh authorities in a neutral and safe location, and he ended his moving appeal with the taditional Buddhist vow "Let All Living Beings Be Happy".

ANNEXURE—XIII

(Report of oppression of the Chakmas as appeared in the Anti-Slavery Reporter, Vol. 13, No. 2 (1985) of The Anti-Slavery Society for the Protection of Human Rights.)

ANTI-SLAVERY

REPORTER

SERIES VII 1985 VOL. 13 No. 2

The Anti-Slavery Society for the Protection of Human Rights

The Chittagong Hill Tracts

The Chakmas are the largest of the minority peoples of the Chittagong Hill Tracts, the remote hilly area in the south of Bangladesh. They are Buddhist in religion and Sino-Tibetan in appearance. Traditionally they have practised shifting cultivation and until about two decades ago they were free from interference by the outside world. Now they are suffering oppression every day and on such a scale that it verges on genocide.

One of the few Chakmas to leave the Tracts lives in Britain but, such are the conditions in his homeland, he must remain anonymous both for his safety and that of his family. He is in touch with the Society and, on one occasion, he wrote :

> ...your article will be very effective and helpful to our campaign.

The Bangladesh Government and the Muslim Bengalis often vociferously criticise the policy of South Africa. At the same time they practise the worst form of racism in the Chittagong Hill Tracts with ferocity and brutality...I believe the international community will not let the Bangladeshi-regime get away with the monstrous crimes it has committed against the defenceless people of the CHT...

I gather that the Bangladesh army and the Muslim Bengali settlers have recently been kidnapping greater number of tribal women than before. They attack the tribal villages during the night and carry off the tribal girls. The tribal people live under extreme fear and terror and they do not dare to speak out about the tyranny of the army in fear of their lives and they have no official and police protection. The Bangladesn army is tightening security measures much more than before.

Finally I would like to express my gratitude to you for all the trouble that you are taking to protect the people of the CHT. They need your help in their just fight for existence.

With best wishes.

It is encouraging to hear from those the Society is trying to help : it is a sign we are not completely crying in the wilderness. His thanks are greatly appreciated and gave much pleasure. The article the unidentifiable Chakma referred to is reproduced here together with a companion piece suggesting his fears were not groundless. Both articles first appeared during 1984 in the London ethnic newspaper, *New World.*

RACISM IN CHITTAGONG

In his column in *New Life* (9 November 1983) Mr A Haque made a very important—and frequently unrecognised—point when he said :

'Possibly a majority of people in any country are prejudiced against their minorities.'

Regrettably, in the land of his forefathers, 600,000 or so people are dying proof that Mr Haque is right—at least in the case of Bangladesh.

There, the 13 tribes of the Chittagong Hill Tracts are different from the majority Bangali Muslim population in many obvious ways. In appearance, they have more in common with the Burmese; in religion, they are mostly Buddhist, and Bengali is not their first language. They are people of the hills and not of the plains; they are not traders but farmers concerned with growing food for their families and not for sale at a profit; and land, which has a special spiritual significance for them, is mostly held in common.

The hillmen of the Chittagong Hill Tracts are conscious of their difference from the Bengalis and cling with pride to their way of life. A way of life it is worth emphasizing, which is in sympathy with nature and which is beneficial to the environment. The tribespeople make up less than one per cent of the total population of Bangladesh and it is the smallness of their numbers which contibutes to their vulnerability. Prejudice thrives on the weakness of minorities and it goes on the rampage when it is condoned—or at least not seen to be actively countered—by a military government.

In March 1980, at the tracts town of Kaokhali Bazar, a small detachment of the Bangladeshi army ordered leading tribespeople to gather in the square and then shot them. The exact number of the dead is not known, but at least 50 people are buried in mass graves at the western corner of Poapara High School, just behind the army camp.

Although matrial law was not imposed on Bangladesh until March 1982, the 5,000 square miles of the hill tracts have been under military rule-undeclared,

"THEY ATTACK THE TRIBAL VILLAGES DURING THE NIGHT AND CARRY OFF THE TRIBAL GIRLS"

illegal but nevertheless real and effective—since "special status" was abolished by Dhaka in 1972.

This status was codified and protected during the days of the British Raj and in fact the tribespeople had a large measure of independence during the Mughal Raj. Until 1964, the hill people had enjoyed wide powers of self-government, had collected their own taxes and run their own police force. Entry into the hills by non-tribespeople had been rigidly controlled and the hillmen had always made up nearly 100 per cent of the population there. Now they are just over half of the people living in the tracts and, if government policy of offering land and other inducements to settlers is not changed, they will soon be outnumbered by Bengalis. They will become a minority not just in Bangladesh, but in their own homelands.

After independence in 1947 and, with increasing speed after 1964, the tribespeople lost control over their land, their lives and their future. Since the 1970s an undeclared but bloody war between them and an alliance of Bangladeshi soldiers and Bengali settlers has been taking place. Since 1976 the number of police stations (manned, of course, by Bengalis) has more than doubled; there are at least 100,000 members of the armed forces in the tracts: checkposts are commonplace and visible evidence of a form of occupation run by the G.O.C. Chittagong. Although settlers are actively encouraged, journalists and visitors are banned.

Bangladesh is a desperately poor and overcrowded country and the promise of "development", especially when made possible by loans from such bodies as the World Bank and Asian Development Bank, must seem irresistable to the bureaucrats of Dhaka. But what is the price of development in human terms?

In 1962 one of the sub-continent's most ambitious hydro-electric schemes was completed at Karnaphuli, deep in the hill tracts. It is the country's major source of electricity, but the electricity bypasses the tribespeople. The artificial lake created behind the dam submerged 40 per cent of the best agricultural land traditionally farmed by the hillmen. The project as a whole displaced 100,000 people, about a sixth of the tribal population. They were not consulted before work began and they were often removed at gunpoint. No one was adequately compensated and many are still waiting for even a token recompense. Most of these families have become landless wanderers as no alternative land was provided for them by the government.

Because the authorities of Bangladesh offer them no protection, the minorities of the Chittagong Hill Tracts are now fighting back and a militia, the Shanti Bahini, is their only on-the-ground defence.

If the unrest in the hill tracts is really just the reaction of people to change which, according to the official stand taken by Dhaka, is for the greater economic good of Bangladesh as a whole, then what is the justification for such acts as the desecration of temples and the attacks on Buddhist priests? Is it progress, an unavoidable by product of development, to slaughter a cow on the saffron robe of a monk? This happened in the Kattali Temple, 70 miles northeast of the hill tracts town of Rangamati.

Economic change is often accompanied by human casualties. But are the almost daily occurrences of rape and bloodshed and arbitrary arrest simply such casualties? Or is something else happening in the Chittagong Hill Tracts?

Alan Whittaker

BANGLADESHI ARMY RAPES AND MURDERS

– Massacre in the Chittagong hill tracts –

Information received by the Anti-Slavery Society confirms that Dhaka is continuing to harass its tribal population to the verge of extinction.

On June 30 this year more than 300 men, women and childern of the Chakma tribe were killed in the Chittagong Hill Tracts by troops of the Bangladeshi military dictatorship.

What seems to have been an officially orchestrated project of provocation and theft was carried out in six tribal villages near the Indian state of Mizoram.

Groups of Bengali 'settlers' arrived suddenly in the ripe paddy fields of the Chakma villagers and began to harvest the rice. They were accompanied by government troops who opened fire when the Chakmas tried to defend their property

The villagers were subsequently rounded up and divided into groups. The men and elderly women were shot out of hand. The girls and young women were repeatedly raped and, when not killed afterwards, forcibly converted to Islam.

The Chakmas and most of the 600,000 original inhabitants of the Chittagong Hill Tracts are Buddhists.

After the massacre 18,000 or so Chakmas fled to the forests of Mizoram. Few have returned because their homes and lands have been plundered and handed over to Bengali newcomers.

Almost all the centuries-old farming land of the original inhabitants of the Tracts is now—as a result of government policy—occupied by Bengalis (poor, illiterate, manipulated) brought in from other districts of Bangladesh.

In August this year (1984), the religious leader of the Chakmas, the Rajguru, The Venerable Aggavansa Mahathero, was a member of the Anti-Slavery Society's delegation to the UN body, the Working Group on Indigenous Populations.

The Rajguru says his people fear to return "Because they have completely lost their faith in the army and people of Bangladesh. The rulers of Bangladesh, including the president, are always disseminating propaganda to mislead the world community; they are falsifying the truth and justifying the falsehood. The Chakmas think their only hope is for the United Nations to take immediate action."

The names of the attacked villages are Chota Harina, Bara Harina, Chedoa, Garjangtali, Soguri Para and Maudong.

The tribal police force was disbanded over 20 years ago so there is no legitimate means of defence for the tribespeople who are scattered over an area the size of Ulster.

The Anti-Slavery Society has reported every year for the past four years to the UN on the ethnocide if not actual genocide of the Chittagong Hill Tracts people.

Alan Whittaker

Comprehensive information on the human rights violations suffered by the minority populations of the Tracts is contained in the Society's publication, *The Chittagong Hill Tracts: militarization, oppression and the hill tribes* Professor Hugh Tinker said of his report : Although this study tells a horrifying tale it is presented in the sober, serious style one expects from its source. The hill tribes have few outside friends; even the technical and economic aid supplied by Western countries has contributed to their ruin.

A.W.

ANNEXURE – XIV

(Names of the Representatives of the Chakma community in District Councils)

(i) *List of Chakma Members in Mizo District Council*

Sl. No.	Name	Constituency	Period/year
1	Medheya Chakma	Nominated member	1952-57
2	Medheya Chakma	Elected from Demagiri	1957-61
3	Hari Kristo Chakma	Elected from Demagiri	1962-70
4	Hari Kristo Chakma	Elected from Demagiri	1970-72

(ii) *List of Chakma members in Pawi Lakher Regional Council*

Sl. No	Name	Period/year
1	Atul Chandra Chakma	1959-64
2	Atul Chandra Chakma	1964-70
3	Atul Chandra Chakma and Arun Kumar Dewan	1970-72

(*iii*) *List of Chakma members in Pawi District Council*

Sl. No	Name	Period/year
1	Arun Kumar Dewan	1972-77
2	Arun Kumar Dewan (Later expelled from the Council due to non-submission of an account of his election expenses and in his place Kartik Ranjan Chakma was elected and raised to the chair of Dy. Chairman)	1977-82
3	Arun Bikash Chakma (subsequently 1982-till date elected to the post of Dy. Chairman.)	

(*iv*) *List of Chairmen of Chakma District Council*

Sl. No.	Name	Period
1	Mayuradhaja Chakma	15.4.1972 to 22.1.1973
2	Chitra Mohan Chakma	23.1.1973 to 18.4.1975
3	Nilomoni Chakma	12.5.1975 to 23.1.1978
4	Ganga Chakma	24.1.1978 to 9.11.1979
5	Bijita Nanda Chakma	26.7.1980 to 16.12.1982
6	Nutan Kumar Chakma	24.1.1983 to December 1985
6	Punya Chakma	December 1985 to 31.12.86

8	Dayal Dhan Chakma	21.4.1987 till date

(*v*) *List of Chief Executive Members of CDC*

Sl. No.	Name	Period/year
1	Atul Chandra Chakma	2.4.72–22.1.73
2	Nilomoni Chakma	23.1.73—16.12.73
3	Sneha Kumar Chakma	17.12.73–1.5.76
4	Laichoka Tongchhunga	2.5.76—14.10.76
5	Administrator's period	15.10.76—23.1.78
6	Nilomoni Chakma	27.1.78–26.1.83
7	Romoni Chakma	27.1.83–19.4.83
8	Pulin Bayan Chakma	21.4.83—30.12.86
9	Nutan Kumar Chakma	31.12.86–till date

ANNEXURE—XV

(Letter of Prof. Suniti Kumar Chatterji containing his views on the status of the Chakma language and the need to preserve it.)

residence :
SUDHARMA
16 Hindusthan Park
Calcutta-29
Phone : 46—1121

Office :
National Library Campus
Belvedere
Calcutta-27
Phone : 45-5319

Suniti Kumar Chatterji
National Professor of India
in Humanities

Dated 23 June, 1967

Among the various forms of Bengali, the Chakma dialect of Chittagong and Chittagong Hill Tracts, which has also spread into Burma, is of very great linguistic importance. It would appear to be a form of South-Eastern Bengali as spoken in Chittagong, but there has been a very widespread phonetic decay or development, and at times along new lines. Then the morphological system also shows some new inflections. Further, the syntax has some special characteristics of its own. The language, compared with any other form of Bengali, appears to be very much abbreviated and attenuated. In its vocabulary there are words from Arakan (Burma), and a number of unexplained words which make its study very tantalising.

Unfortunately very little has been done in the study of Chakma. Excepting one or two small monographs or notes there has been no serious work in the language. It has become just a village patois and has no real literature to boast of. There are some songs and poems of a popular nature, partly religious and partly narrative, and excepting for two books which were collected and published by Sri Tripur Chandra Sen, no printed literature is available using the Bengali script. Through the influence of the Bhikkhus from among the Chakma people, who used to have their training in Buddhism and Pali in Burma, the Burmese script along with Pali manuscript was introduced among the Chakmas some generations ago. They were cut off from the main trend of Bengali literature, and in their isolation some of them employed a kind of simplified Burmese script to write their Bengali dialect. Some literature in this Burmese-Chakma Bengali is found in manuscript writing, and already with a view to bringing out books in Burmese-Chakma an enterprising Publisher had a fount of these special Burmese-Chakma script cast for the language. But as this is very recondite, and as it is not at all popular, it is fast going out of use, and excepting for a few old people nobody can write it. The best proposition for the Chakma dialect would be to write it in Bengali characters as it has been done successfully.

As students of Bengali and Indo-Aryan linguistics, we are very much interested in the development of Chakma studies. One or more Chakma young man or woman with a knowledge of the language as it is spoken, combined with a good knowledge of Bengali as well as English should immediately take up the task of preserving this language for posterity by both study and publication of texts in it. There is no lack of highly edudated and cultured peoples among the Chakma speakers including some members of the landed aristocracy as well as men in the professions. Just to perpetuate a knowledge of their home dialect, they should form themselves into an association for the preservation and development of Chakma (Chakma-Bhasha-Prabardhini Samiti).

I would suggest that some of the young men and women studying for higher degrees in Calcutta should form themselves into a study-Group and start collecting materials in Chakma, both such specimens of folk-poetry and folk-literature as can be gleaned from among the older generations and also by creating a literature of translations from standard Bengali or other languages into Chakma. But the more important thing would be to preserve the language by its study and by gathering the floating material which is on the way to passing into oblivion.

I trust that the leaders of the Chakma community in Bengal and elsewhere will pay serious attention to this matter and find out ways and means to keep up a study of their language which is unique among the dialects of Bengali for some of its intrinsic characters and qualities.

Sd/-
(Suniti Kumar Chatterji)
Emeritus Professor of Comparative Philology,
University of Calcutta
Ex-Chairman, West Bengal Legislative Council
and National Professor of India in Humanities.

Index

Maps and Illustrations

1. Prime Minister, Rajiv Gandhi, at Demagiri (Mizoram) while addressing the people during his visit

2. Smt. Indira Gandhi, Late Prime Minister of India, in Chakma Traditional dress with Shri Hari Kristo Chakma, M.L.A. (Right)

3. Late Prime Minister Indira Gandhi, in Traditional Chakma drers with Mr. Pulin Bayan Chakma, C.E.M. of Chakma District Council (Extreme right)

4. His Excellency Hiteswar Saikia, Governor of Mizoram

5. Mr. Laldenga, Chief Minister, Mizoram

(b) (a) (c) (d) (e)

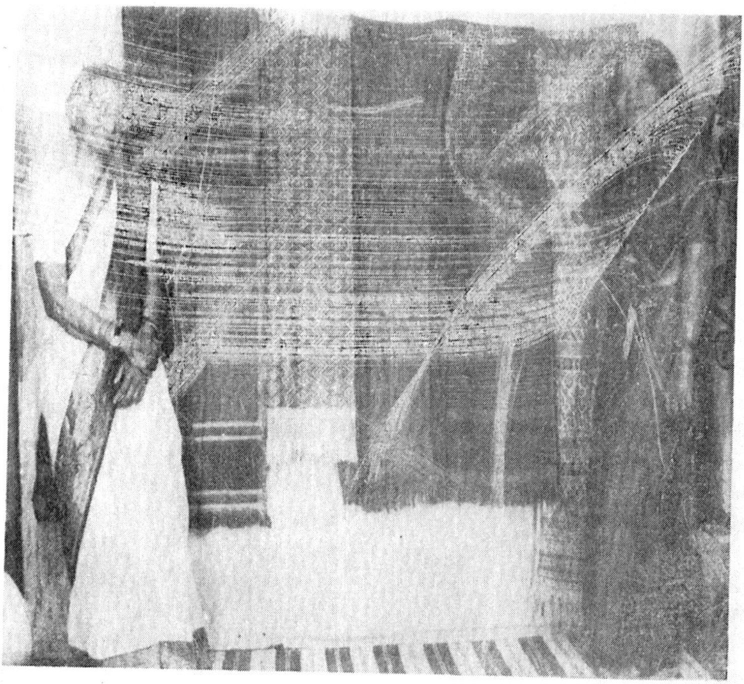

6. Chakma Khadi Alam (Pattern)

A. Chakma Khadi, upper part of Girl's dress.

B. Chakma Lady (Author's Mother) in Sari

C. Hand Woven Table Covers by Chakma Girls

D. Chakma Alam (Pattern)

E. Chakma Girl in Traditional dress

7. Chakma Belle with Traditional ornaments

8. Chakma Belle at River Ghat (Kamalanagar)

9. Cultural Programme in Nunsuri Village (20.11.1986.)

10. Chakma M.L.A. welcoming Smt. Indira Gandhi on her arrival at Aijawl

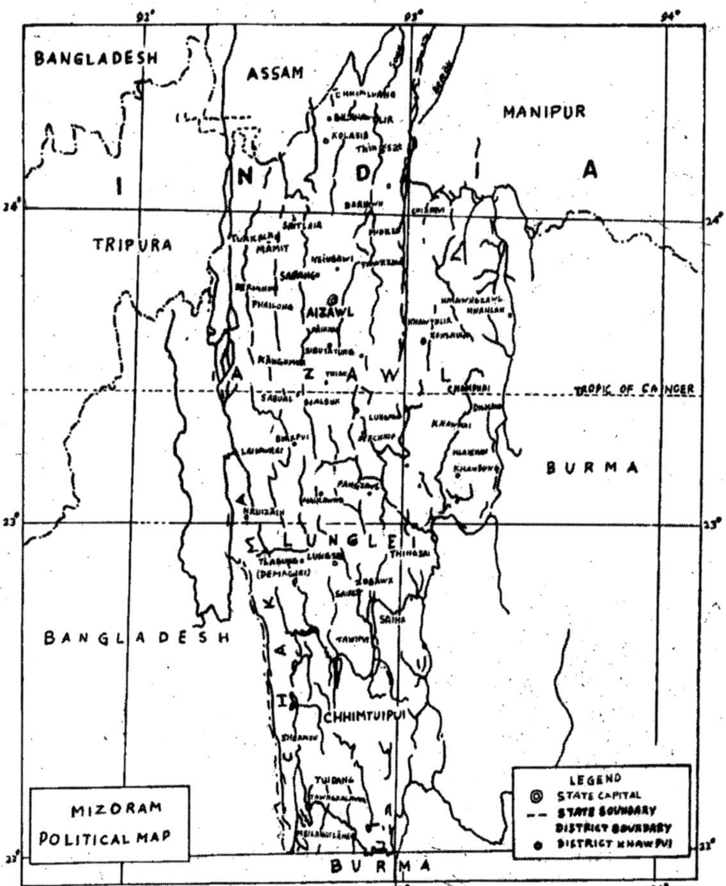
BANGLADESH
ASSAM
MANIPUR
I N D I A
TRIPURA
AIZAWL
A I Z A W L
TROPIC OF CANCER
BURMA
L U N G L E I
BANGLADESH
CHHIMTUIPUI
LEGEND
STATE CAPITAL
STATE BOUNDARY
DISTRICT BOUNDARY
DISTRICT KHAWPUI
MIZORAM
POLITICAL MAP
B U R M A

Fig.1

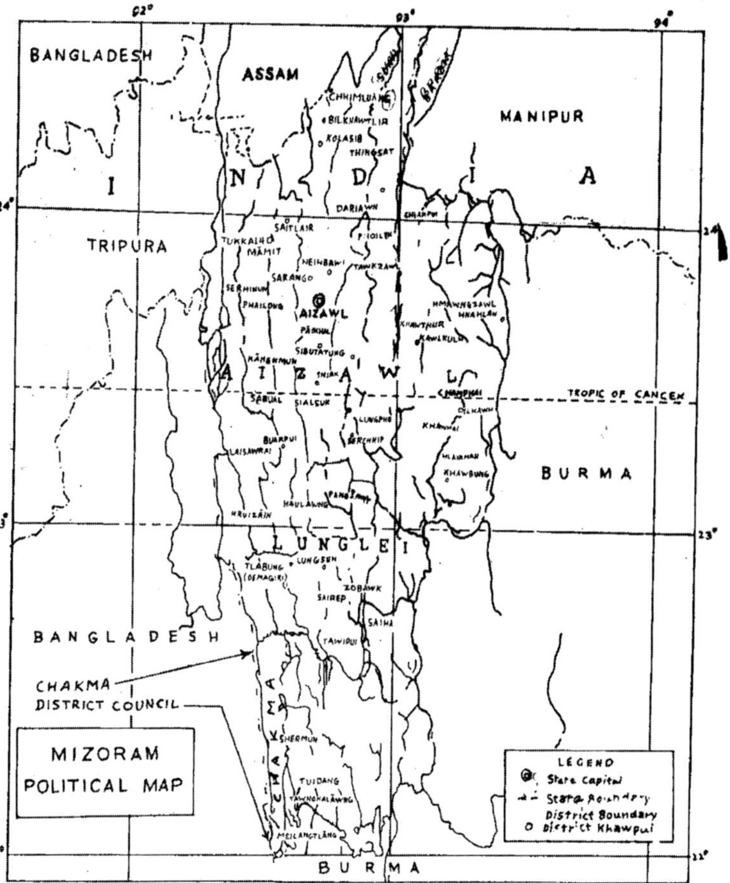
BANGLADESH
ASSAM
MANIPUR
I N D I A
TRIPURA
AIZAWL
A I Z A W L
TROPIC OF CANCER
BURMA
L U N G L E I
BANGLADESH
CHAKMA
DISTRICT COUNCIL
CHAKMA
MIZORAM
POLITICAL MAP
LEGEND
State Capital
State Boundary
District Boundary
District Khawpui
B U R M A

Fig.2

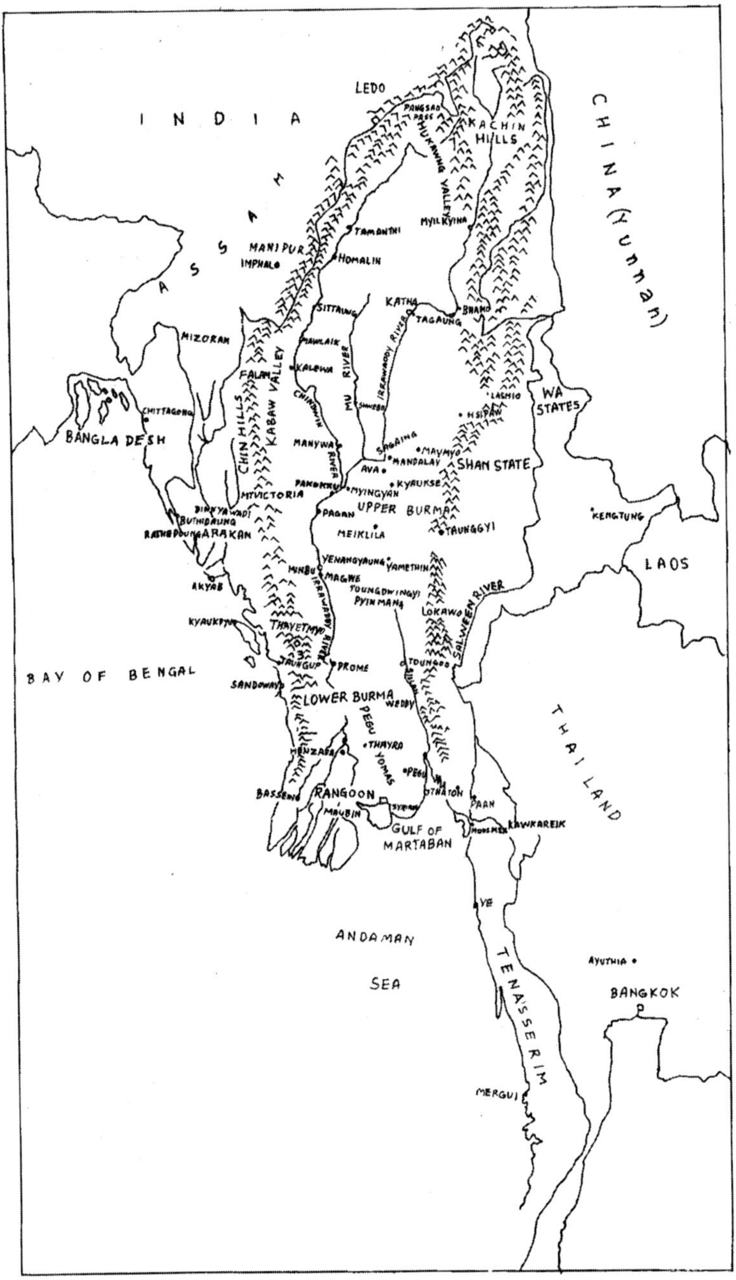
INDIA
LEDO
ASSAM
MANIPUR
IMPHAL
KACHIN HILLS
CHINA (YUNNAN)
HUKAWNG VALLEY
TAMANTHI
MYITKYINA
HOMALIN
KATHA
TAGAUNG
BHAMO
SITTAUNG
MIZORAM
MAWLAIK
KALEWA
FALAM
CHIN HILLS
KABAW VALLEY
MU RIVER
IRRAWADDY RIVER
CHINDWIN RIVER
CHITTAGONG
BANGLA DESH
LASHIO
HSIPAW
WA STATES
SAGAING
MAYMYO
MANDALAY
SHAN STATE
MANYWA
AVA
KYAUKSE
MYINGYAN
MT VICTORIA
UPPER BURMA
PAGAN
BUTHIDAUNG
ARAKAN
MEIKTILA
TAUNGGYI
KENGTUNG
LAOS
YENANGYAUNG
YAMETHIN
MINBU
MAGWE
AKYAB
PYINMANA
SALWEEN RIVER
LOKAWO
KYAUKPYU
THAYETMYO
TAUNGUP
PROME
TOUNGOO
BAY OF BENGAL
SANDOWAY
LOWER BURMA
PEGU YOMAS
THAILAND
THAYRA
HENZADA
PEGU
BASSEIN
RANGOON
THATON
PAAN
MAUBIN
SYRIAM
GULF OF MARTABAN
KAWKAREIK
YE
ANDAMAN SEA
TENASSERIM
AYUTHIA
BANGKOK
MERGUI

Fig.6

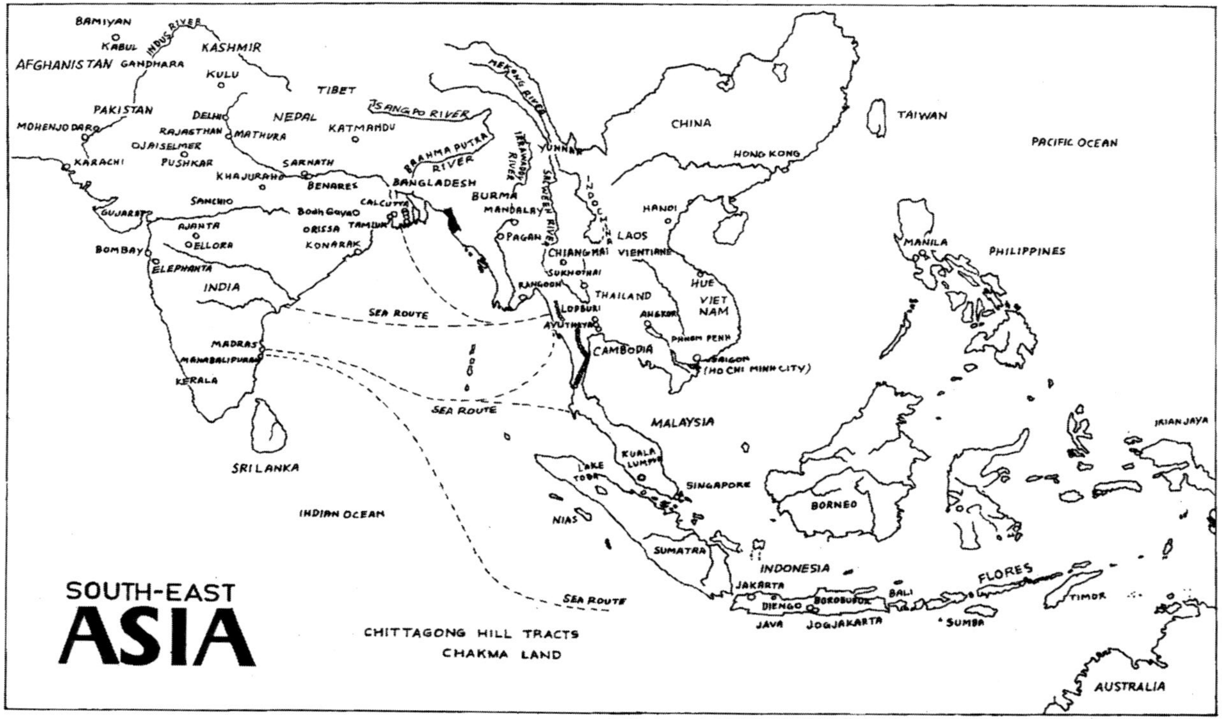
SOUTH-EAST
ASIA
BAMIYAN
KABUL
INDUS RIVER
KASHMIR
AFGHANISTAN
GANDHARA
KULU
TIBET
PAKISTAN
DELHI
NEPAL
TSANGPO RIVER
MOHENJODARO
RAJASTHAN
MATHURA
KATMANDU
JAISELMER
KARACHI
PUSHKAR
SARNATH
BRAHMAPUTRA RIVER
KHAJURAHO
BENARES
BANGLADESH
SANCHIO
CALCUTTA
GUJARAT
AJANTA
Bodh Gaya
ORISSA
TAMLUK
ELLORA
KONARAK
BOMBAY
ELEPHANTA
INDIA
MADRAS
MAHABALIPURAM
KERALA
SRI LANKA
INDIAN OCEAN
SEA ROUTE
SEA ROUTE
SEA ROUTE
MEKONG RIVER
IRRAWADDY RIVER
YUNNAN
SALWEEN RIVER
BURMA
MANDALAY
PAGAN
INDOCHINA
CHIANGMAI
SUKHOTHAI
RANGOON
LOPBURI
AYUTHAYA
THAILAND
LAOS
VIENTIANE
HANOI
HUE
VIET NAM
ANGKOR
PHNOM PENH
CAMBODIA
SAIGON (HO CHI MINH CITY)
CHINA
HONG KONG
TAIWAN
PACIFIC OCEAN
MANILA
PHILIPPINES
MALAYSIA
KUALA LUMPUR
LAKE TOBA
SINGAPORE
NIAS
SUMATRA
BORNEO
INDONESIA
JAKARTA
DIENGO
BOROBUDUR
JAVA
JOGJAKARTA
BALI
SUMBA
FLORES
TIMOR
IRIAN JAYA
AUSTRALIA
CHITTAGONG HILL TRACTS
CHAKMA LAND

Fig.7